An Australian Country Life

An Australian Country Life

A Portrait of
Bobbie Maple-Brown

PETER TAYLOR

ALLEN & UNWIN
Sydney London Boston

First published in 1986
Allen & Unwin Australia Pty Ltd
8 Napier Street, North Sydney, NSW 2060, Australia

Allen & Unwin New Zealand Limited
60 Cambridge Terrace, Wellington, New Zealand

George Allen & Unwin (Publishers) Ltd
18 Park Lane, Hemel Hempstead, Herts HP2 4TE England

Allen & Unwin Inc.
8 Winchester Place, Winchester, Mass 01890 USA

National Library of Australia
Cataloguing-in-Publication
Taylor, Peter.
An Australian country life.
ISBN 0 04 920103 4.

1. Maple-Brown, Bobbie. 2. Sheep ranchers — New South
Wales — Goulburn Region — Biography. 3. Country life —
New South Wales — Goulburn Region. 4. Goulburn Region
(N.S.W.) — Biography. I. Title.
994.4'7

Library of Congress Catalog Card Number 86-71307

Set in 11/13pt Goudy Old Style by Meredith Typesetters
Printed by Singapore National Printers (Pte) Ltd. in Singapore.

Contents

Prologue

'I WAS about seven, I think. I was out in the sulky with my sister Hazel and our governess and we were driving across the flat near the river.

'Well, you know how children can make a game out of anything. I mean, driving in the sulky across the river flats was not very exciting to us at that time. So we imagined that our husbands were in another sulky alongside us and we started to race them. That was much more exciting. We whipped up the horse and kept looking over our shoulder at the husbands we were leaving behind.

'Then, before we knew what was happening, the horse tried to jump over a three-rail fence, close to one of the gates which we should have opened. Well, I knew I couldn't do much about it, so I closed my eyes and waited for it to happen.

'The horse managed to scramble over the fence, but the sulky got stuck on the top rail. My sister and the governess were thrown out on one side and I was thrown out on the other. When I opened my eyes I was curled up in a little ball just behind the horse's hooves. The others were both crying and I was very ashamed because I didn't seem able to cry. I thought I would get into trouble and they wouldn't.

'A man saw what had happened (he was here until the 1940s), and he managed to get the sulky off the fence. The horse was not hurt and neither were we, which was very lucky.

'But then we had to go and tell father, and we were terrified of that. People always said they would tell father if we did anything wrong, but they rarely did. But we knew there was no way out this time. He was reading his paper in the smoking room and we had to tell him what had happened. When we had finished he asked us if anybody had been hurt. We just stood there and said no. Then my aunt came in and said, "Well, dears, I think you had better go home for tea".

'So we did. When mother asked us what had happened I said, "Dad didn't say anything, but Aunt Flory was very nice".'

Introduction

I FIRST MET Bobbie Maple-Brown in 1982 when I visited Springfield as part of my research for a book called *Pastoral Properties of Australia*.

She was a very remarkable lady. She was perceptive, charming, full of character and, to my surprise, very funny. I wrote later:

'That evening Bobbie Maple-Brown comes to the homestead to celebrate her eighty-third birthday. She lives in a modern house about half a kilometre from the homestead, stoutly maintaining that she has not retired.

'The family is assembled in the drawing room as a car glides up the gravel drive and sighs to a halt outside the big french windows. Bobbie comes in cursing the stick she has to use to climb the steps and settles herself into a settee that she has known all her life. She is trying to give up smoking and says that she has brought only three cigarettes and three matches. When she unwraps the present from Mary, the cook, she is delighted to find two packets of cigarettes but is left with the problem of having only three matches. I give her mine.

'In the dining room the huge mahogany table is lit by candles and the light barely reaches the corners of the room. The jackeroo tries to work out which knife and fork he should use for each dish and Bobbie tells me a story that would take any radio station immediately off the air.'

The truth was that I burst into an eruption of laughter that I had much difficulty controlling. Not only was it a very good story, but it was told with such a straight face that the end caught me completely unawares. I remember thinking that if I could do the same when I was eighty-three I would have little to complain about.

After *Pastoral Properties of Australia* was published I was asked to write a history of Springfield that would commemorate one hundred and fifty years of stud merino breeding there. I agreed happily. Springfield has been in the hands of the same family during the whole of that time and I knew the story to be worth telling.

As part of the research for that book I had a number of long conversations with Bobbie. She had, after all, been born at Springfield and had lived all but twenty-one years of her life there. No-one knew the place better than she did and she had information that could not be found anywhere else.

But as these conversations went on I began to realise that what Bobbie was telling me was of much wider significance than the history of Springfield. She was telling me about a way of life which was long gone, she was telling me about how people behaved, how they thought and what they did. More particularly, she was telling me about the wealthy and secure life she had lived, first as a grazier's daughter and then as a grazier's wife. And it was not always what I expected.

Although Bobbie Maple-Brown was born into wealth and privilege, and enjoyed both as much as most of us would, she saw injustice and tried to correct it. She saw a class structure that was in many ways more rigid than that in England, and thought it idiotic. Others saw these things too, of course. But what makes Bobbie remarkable was that she was on the 'inside'. She showed a degree of caring, of concern, of responsibility that have not been part of the popular concept of the grazier's life. There is no doubt that some graziers cared nothing for such things, but it became clear that the Faithfulls and Maple-Browns were not among them. She was ahead of her time in many ways and I have no doubt that she shocked many people, often without even realising it, but what she was telling me threw new light on this aspect of rural life.

When I suggested to Bobbie that what she was telling me was worth publishing she was surprised and hesitant. Surprised because she could see nothing unusual in the life she had lived and thought it could not possibly be of interest to anybody else. It was, she said, just an ordinary life which had simply gone on longer than most. And hesitant because she would be embarrassed if those who knew her thought she was pushing herself forward as a rather special person. She was not special, she said.

But Bobbie Maple-Brown's life covers more than a third of European history in Australia. True, she was never close to the big events, but she was an accurate observer of countless small ones.

This book, then, is about those small events. Some are curious, some are funny and some had no significance except to those they affected. But they were all part of a country life that was changing more rapidly than it ever had before, and they show aspects of it that are in danger of being forgotten.

This is not a history book, nor does it pretend to be a biography. It is an account of a life that was lived in circumstances that few enjoyed then, and which are almost extinct now. But above all it is an account of an ordinary Australian who thinks she is far from special.

I will leave you to be the judge of that.

PETER TAYLOR
Sydney, 1986

1
Childhood

FLORENCE FAITHFULL was born on 18 November 1899. She was the second daughter of Lucian and Ethel Faithfull and she was born on the family property of Springfield, not far from Goulburn in New South Wales.

Springfield was one of the oldest properties in the district and, by then, one of the most successful. It had first been taken up by William Pitt Faithfull in 1827 when the country was an untouched plain and Goulburn had not yet been founded. His sister had recently married Dr Gibson and they had already settled on a grant nearby which they called Terranna.

It was beautiful country. The plain was vast and lightly timbered and the Mulwaree Chain of Ponds promised permanent water even in the driest seasons. Beyond the plain a range of hills rose to define the extent of it and provided a distant backdrop which was blue and shimmering in the summer heat. But in the cold of winter the same hills would often have a coating of snow and at Springfield even the water in the troughs could freeze solid overnight.

This was grazing country. Sheep country. After a modest beginning William Pitt Faithfull built up a large flock of Saxon merinos and in 1838 Springfield became a stud. Soon, it became more than that. It became a village. It had to. Although Goulburn was by now a thriving country town it was nearly twenty kilometres away and the round trip took more than half a day.

In the centre of this village William Pitt Faithfull built his first modest house. Then in the 1840s, with Springfield prosperous and well established, he started to build a much grander house alongside. His plan was to build a number of extensions, but by the time he had finished they had simply absorbed the original house to make an impressive double-storeyed homestead of nearly forty rooms. It was the 'big house'.

William Faithfull and his wife Mary Deane had six sons and three daughters. In time, two of the daughters, Constance and Lilian, moved away, leaving only Aunt Flory at Springfield. Most of the sons moved away too, and in the end it was the youngest, Augustus Lucian, who stayed behind to help his father. By the 1870s Lucian Faithfull was already a sheep breeder of note and the running of Springfield was largely in his hands.

Lucian Faithfull married Ethel Joplin, daughter of a Goulburn bank manager, in 1895. He had selected a site for a new house some time earlier and had already planted the trees which were to give it its name — Pinea. But with his father in poor health, and with Pinea more than a kilometre from the big house, he had to abandon that idea and instead he built his new house in a paddock just beyond the garden hedge. It was called the Cottage.

Mary Deane had died in 1889 and when William Pitt Faithfull died in 1896 he left Springfield to Lucian — except for the big house and the extensive gardens around it. These he left to his daughters for as long as they lived, after which they would become part of Springfield once more. So Lucian Faithfull and his family continued to live at the Cottage while his sister Florence lived alone as a spinster in the big house.

His father had been a pioneer, but Lucian Faithfull was now a grazier, for times had changed. Wool was then the key to the economy of Australia, and those who produced it were important people. They had land, they had substance, they employed many people and if their individual role in the national economy was slight, their role in the local economy was overwhelming. It is not surprising that some saw themselves as the landed gentry of Australia.

Lucian Faithfull did not. Certainly he recognised his importance locally, for he could hardly escape that, but he was also aware that wealth that came from the land was fragile. He knew that many potential 'dynasties' failed in the second or third generations and, although Springfield flourished under his care, he refused to take it for granted.

But these were private thoughts. The world that Florence Faithfull joined that day in 1899 was secure, established and wealthy. The wealth was not flamboyant, indeed at times it was almost invisible, but it was always there. And if Lucian thought it might be temporary, hardly anybody else did.

Lucian Faithfull's more immediate concern, however, was that his second child was, like his first, a daughter. What he really needed was a son who would eventually take over Springfield just as he had done from his father. When his third, and last, child turned out to be a daughter too nobody wanted to be the one to tell him. So they sent the cook to give him the news.

Although his second child was a girl, she was soon given a boy's name. She was christened Florence but she was called Bobbie by her family. Not, though, by the staff: to them she was 'Miss Florence', and remained so until she married. Years later one of her grandchildren said she could not bear to be called Miss because she thought it made her seem old. 'But I didn't see anything old about it. I was called Miss by the people on the place from when I was five or six and I never connected it with age. But that has gone out of date now. Really it was going out of date when my son was born. I suggested to the staff that they call him Mr Jim, and so they didn't call him anything for a long time.'

The three sisters, Hazel, Bobbie and Valerie, enjoyed a childhood that was privileged even then and almost non existent now. There were only two firm rules. One was that they must not tell lies, and the other was that they must not be late for meals. 'You had the staff, you see, and you couldn't keep them waiting.'

One day, though, they did. Riding beyond the nearest hills, they saw the road to Lake George. 'So we decided to ride to the Lake. We didn't get back until after seven o'clock, which was well after dinner time, so we got into trouble for that. We would have ridden eighty or ninety kilometres that day, I think. It makes me laugh now when the children say their ponies are tired after they've cantered them a few times around the paddock!'

They spent a great deal of their time riding. Bobbie, like her elder sister, was taught to ride side-saddle, but they soon gave that up, and nobody objected. The clothes were the problem. Hazel had been fitted out with a long riding habit which was very smart, but she ruined that when sliding down a railway embankment. And petticoats had an even shorter life. 'We tore those when we were climbing and the punishment was to lie on our back while the nurse mended it.'

Giving up the unequal struggle, their mother used some strong galatea to make them each a tunic and a pair of bloomers to go underneath. They were almost indestructible, as Bobbie soon found out. 'I had climbed a tree and as I went to jump off I got hooked up by my galatea bloomers. Hazel kept telling me to bounce up and down to tear them, but they wouldn't. In the end a gardener had to get a ladder and unhook me. I could never face him after that.'

They rode naturally rather than precisely, with a style closer to that of a bushman rather than that of the show ring. But it was effective. One of their games was Bobbies and Bushies. 'One person was given a start and you had to chase them and catch them up. If you were the one in front you would jump your horse over a pile of logs and hope that those behind you would be too frightened to go over it.'

Another favourite was the paperchase, where they followed a trail of paper in an attempt to catch up with the person who was laying it. It was not as easy as it sounds. On one of them, across the Gundary Plain, Bobbie was leading the pack when she came to a waterhole. She could see the paper trail continuing on the other side but a boy nearby warned her that it was a trap. The water there was quite deep, he said, and the real crossing was further down. 'I called out to my sister, who was coming up behind me, and then looked round. Splosh! There she was in the middle of the river. She wasn't going to go the long way round!'

But horses were not simply for recreation. They were, in Bobbie's early years at least, transport as well. In 1888 William Pitt Faithfull had ordered a carriage to be built by Brewsters in New York for the considerable sum of US$2000. It was to be a landau 'with a small window at the back, the metal work to be made of silver and the lining to be of green cloth and morocco combined. The wheels will have a broad black stripe with edging of thin lines of red which will make a rich and quiet effect'. The price also included harness with silver fittings and the family crest was to be mounted in silver on the blinkers. 'All,' said Brewsters, 'to be of the very best in every respect, but plain and nothing gaudy.'

This carriage arrived in 1889 and had been in use ever since. Indeed, Lucian and his new wife had returned to Springfield in it after their honeymoon in 1895. Later, it became Aunt Flory's carriage, and

Bobbie Faithfull on her mother's knee, with her elder sister, Hazel.

that is how Bobbie remembers it. When it was needed the coachman brought it to the front door of the big house and then they would go down the long drive to join the road to Goulburn.

The horses would move at a trot except when going uphill, when they would walk. It took an hour and a half to reach Goulburn, a journey which now takes fifteen minutes by car. Even so, the coachman was notoriously slow. One of Bobbie's cousins once said to him that they had to be in Goulburn by a certain time and look what it was already. 'Well, miss,' he said, 'if it's as late as that now there's no use hurrying.'

On another occasion they were returning from Goulburn on a cold winter's night when the coachman saw the lights of a car approaching in the distance. He stopped the coach and made them all get out, then turned the horses round so they could not see the approaching lights. When the car had passed they climbed back into the coach and continued their cold, slow journey back to Springfield.

Although the coach could be completely covered by two large hoods and had the benefit of American springs, it was not very comfortable to ride in. It was, of course, even more uncomfortable to drive. The coachman sat on an open box behind the horses with no protection from the weather. He wore a large coat and gloves and wrapped a rug over his knees as well, but they did little to keep out the biting wind or heavy rain.

Motor cars were rare at that time, but it was not long before there was one at Springfield. One night, when Bobbie was about five, she heard a strange noise and climbed out of bed to investigate. Looking through the window she saw the lights of a car coming up the drive and heard the excited clamour of the grown-ups as they went outside to meet it. Her father had driven it from Sydney with his newly appointed chauffeur sitting beside him.

That first car was called a Swift Sure, but in reality it was neither swift nor sure. The tyres were the main problem. On roads that were still quite unsuitable for motor vehicles, punctures were a constant problem and repairing them could delay any journey. 'We used to wonder whether we might get home or not. If we were at the side of the road with a puncture people would go past in their buggies and think, "Well, at least we know we'll get there with a buggy, but these cars . . ."'

Uncertain though it might be, that first car was warmly welcomed by her mother. Although she had then lived at Springfield for ten years she remained a town person at heart and the infrequent visits to Goulburn were important to her. Infrequent because they were necessarily lengthy, and because they required the use of the coach, two horses, and the coachman. Nor could they be made in the rain because the coachman insisted that it would ruin the harness. The car, then, provided a freedom that she had not enjoyed before.

There was already a school at Springfield, but it was not proper for Bobbie and her sisters to attend it. It was run by a gentleman teacher called Mr Finley and it provided a basic education for the children of station workers and those from other properties nearby. Some of these had to ride about ten kilometres each way and during the day they kept their horses in a small yard next to the tiny schoolhouse.

Although the girls did not attend this school they were, as members of the Faithfull family, required to take part in some of its activities. And none were more important than the sports day. It was held every year on Empire Day — 'We don't have that now, do we? You are not allowed to have an empire' — and it took place down on the flats near the school.

Races were run and prizes were given and the athletic pecking order was established for the coming year. Bobbie and her sisters took part, but she was already aware that they were different. 'I was horrified once because Mr Finley put my younger sister such a long way in front at the start of a race. It was a handicap affair, you know, and I thought that was terrible. I don't think she won it even then because she was still very little. I would have felt even worse if she had.'

They were, of course, dressed for a social occasion, not an athletic one. 'You wore a dress. Not your best dress, your second best dress, I think. The best dress you had one year was your second best dress the next year. And we wore a hat and usually a coat because it was winter.' The station girls usually had only one good dress, and that is what they wore.

The prizes were very simple and were usually made by people on the station. Bobbie's nurse once dressed a doll as a prize, but that was very special. Usually Mr Finley ended the proceedings by throwing a handful of unwrapped sweets into the paddock and the children, whooping and shouting and totally indifferent to hygiene, scrambled after them.

There was, however, another station activity which was much more frequent and far more important: church.

Every two weeks the vicar came out from Goulburn to hold a service in the church room inside the big house. The station people filed in through a side door and when they had all arrived the Faithfull family entered through a door from the dining room. 'It was so feudal, wasn't it? They used to sit on benches, well they were pews really, and we sat facing them. Mother and father sat on a sofa and we snuggled between them. Everybody was in their best clothes, of course, and it was all very serious. At least it was supposed to be. Dad used to make faces at us sometimes and we had to try not to laugh. It was all very confusing. But wasn't it wrong to make such a terrible difference between people? We sat on the sofa and they sat in pews.'

School for Bobbie Faithfull meant a governess, but even that didn't start until she was seven. The schoolroom was in the Cottage and from then on part of each weekday had to be spent doing lessons. One governess, indeed, announced that she would teach them Sunday school as well. 'We were very indignant about that. Then Hazel said that we would go into the bush at the back of the house and that if we heard her ring the bell we had to go in, but if we didn't hear it we were free. I thought that was a very silly idea. If we were going to run away we might as well stay away and have done with it. But that is how we did it. If we heard the bell, we went back.'

2

Growing Up

THE COTTAGE that Lucian Faithfull had built in 1895 was, in spite of its name, now a large and rambling house with many rooms. Lucian Faithfull was an enthusiastic builder. He had added a dining room, another kitchen, a maid's bedroom, and then two complete wings. The front part of the original bluestone house was still as he had built it, but because he would never knock a hole in the wall to make another door his extensions rambled away to make three sides of a courtyard at the back. These rooms were entered from a covered verandah which ran along all three sides.

In the middle of a Goulburn winter this was far from luxurious. There were no fires in the bedrooms, no hot water bottles unless they were ill, and the only way of going to bed warm was to have a bath first and then run quickly along the open verandah to the bedroom. The only relief came if they had visitors, or if they were visiting one of their cousins.

'If we had friends to stay then we had a fire in the bedroom because mother thought people from Sydney would feel the cold. And when I stayed with a friend near Braidwood it was very comfortable. The maid came in every morning and lit the fire before you got up. It went out during the day but the maid lit it again in the evening. We had none of

The cottage at Springfield where Bobbie grew up. She returned to live here after the death of her father in 1942.

that at home. But our maid did bring a jug of hot water each evening so you could wash your hands, and then turned down the bed.'

For a time she even had to sleep in the summer house for the 'fresh air', even in winter. It was an attractive building with roses growing over the roof, but the sides were open to the weather. 'It was bad enough in the winter, but the summer was worse because I was terrified there might be a snake in the bed. They only laughed and said of course there wouldn't be. But there could have been, couldn't there?' Fortunately there never was.

Being so far from Goulburn, and unable to mix with the station children, they had to make their own amusements and keep their own company. On Bobbie's fourth birthday, for example, there were only nineteen guests, and one of those was a girl from Goulburn who had her thirteenth birthday on the same day. Four of the guests were boys and all were killed during the First World War.

Nor did she have much contact with her father. He had been forty-three when she was born and he never seemed to know what to do with girls. 'If you had been a boy,' he said once in a rare moment of anger, 'I would have whipped you.' Instead, he could only walk away in confusion.

It was many years before Bobbie got to know him well. At that time he was more of a figurehead than a father, a remote symbol of ultimate authority. Even when they were on holiday they saw little of him.

They used to go to Manly for three weeks every year and always stayed at the same hotel right on the beach. Their mother used to take them swimming, although many people then thought that was not very nice because it was mixed bathing. Their mother thought it was all right so long as they all wore stockings. 'She always wore long black stockings under a bathing suit that was like a dress. She'd often get knocked over by the surf and we would see her black legs waving about in the air and we would have to go and pull her out.'

Lucian Faithfull took no part in this. Instead he caught the ferry over to the city each morning and spent the day at the Australian Club. 'I don't think he cared much for the beach.'

Visits from cousins were always welcome for the variety they brought. They could be shown the surrounding country in rides that took all day, there were stories to tell and new ones to listen to, and boisterous games that came from nothing.

One favourite was to chase each other through the big house. It was possible at that time to make a complete circuit by going up one staircase, passing through the bathroom to an outside balcony, and then coming down the main staircase to finish in a lobby next to the front hall. It was even more fun when they split into two groups and did it in opposite directions.

Aunt Flory, living there alone, must have had more patience than most. If not actually strict, she was very much a product of the Victorian Age. She took her meals sitting alone at the huge mahogany table in the dining room and the maids brought each course from the kitchen which was far away at the back of the house. They then waited outside the door, or sat on the steps if they thought she wouldn't see them, and waited for her to ring the bell for the next course. The rest of the time she spent in the library, a small room off the front hall which earned its title because there was a bookcase on either side of the fireplace.

The gardens around the house supplied the rest of the family with fruit and fresh vegetables, but apart from that Aunt Flory had almost nothing to do with the running of the property. Her main duty, and that only occasionally, was to entertain visiting ram buyers to lunch. But she never did that in her dining room.

Although the big house had once been very lively — when Lucian was growing up there were regularly thirteen people for breakfast — now only her nieces made a noise.

'She was marvellous really. She was pretty old by then but she just sat in the library while we raced around and she never once told us to be quiet. One New Year's Eve we went over there with tin cans and whistles and went up the stairs so we could get out on to the roof. As we went past her room she popped her head out and asked us what was happening and we all said, "Happy New Year, Aunt Flory!" "Oh, is that all, dear," she said, and went back to bed. When we were on the roof we made a tremendous racket because we thought New Year's Eve was very exciting. One of the gardeners even fired his gun. We weren't sure whether he was joining in or trying to get us to stop!'

And when the noisy games came to an end there were always stories to tell, chilling stories told in whispers as they huddled together in the schoolroom at the Cottage late at night. Most were 'make-up' stories, some had been heard from other people, and some, a few, were true. Ghost stories and snake stories were the best, although Bobbie much preferred ghost stories. 'I could always think that I didn't believe in ghosts, but I couldn't think that about snakes.'

Nor, in truth, was she all that sure about ghosts. For one of the true stories belonged to her. It started one Michaelmas holiday when she was about twelve. She was teaching another girl to ride a bicycle and they were practising by riding along the drive to the main gate on the Goulburn road. On the way back Bobbie was ahead of the other girl when she saw a tall black figure beside the drive. She said 'Good evening', but got no reply. 'I thought it was strange. It was just straight up and down. Not headless, but as if it had something over its head.'

When she got to the next gate she waited for the girl to catch up with her, and then asked her if she had seen a tall black figure. She hadn't, so they both went back to see if it was still there. But there was no sign of it and they thought no more about it.

During the Michaelmas holiday the following year she was with another cousin and they were sitting on a gate waiting for the others to come back down the drive with the bicycles. They both heard rustling

Picnic in the garden at Springfield. Lucian Faithfull with his wife and sisters.

in the grass and then saw a black figure cross the drive just in front of them. The other girl said how strange it was that they had not heard the sound of feet on the gravel, and Bobbie told her what had happened the previous year. Her cousin was reluctant to go any further, but when the others brought the bicycles back she agreed to go and Bobby gave her a push to start her off.

They had not gone far when they saw the figure again. This time it was making its way up the hill towards the family vault which William Pitt Faithfull had built and where he was now buried. This was too much for the other girl, who promptly screamed and fell off the bike. 'I put her back on the bike and pushed her to get her going, and she came pedalling home as fast as she could and so did I.'

It was a compelling story when told in the darkness of the schoolroom. It led them all to agree that when they died they would come back and visit those who were still alive. But the next day Bobbie sought out one of the boys. 'Look,' she said, 'if you die first, would you mind coming back in the daylight?'

That boy did die first. At Gallipoli.

3

England and Europe

T HE NEWS was so exciting that Bobbie and Hazel could hardly believe it. Their father had just told them that they would all be going to England! It was 1914, and they were to leave in March. It would be a long trip, perhaps even a year, and the only flaw as far as Bobbie was concerned was that she would probably have to spend some of that time at school.

But that really did not matter. At least, not then. The prospect of seeing all those wonderful places was too intoxicating to be marred by something as ordinary as going to school. She already knew a great deal about England. Her mother's family were English and she had learnt much from her, and her father regularly received magazines from England which were rich with engraved pictures.

The family would, in fact, be 'going home', even though none of them had been born there. Indeed, the Faithfull family had been in Australia far longer than most as the founder, William Pitt's father, William Faithfull, had landed in Sydney in 1791 as a private in the New South Wales Corps. But England was still 'home'.

'I was always proud of being an Australian, but I also thought of myself as British. That is what it said on your passport. So we never thought of ourselves as foreigners and we really did think Britain was our home. Even in 1965 I talked of "going home", and the person who was with me said, "What on earth are you saying that for? It's not home". Of course, I've quite given it up now, but we didn't think we were putting on airs then. It was just a natural thing.'

Bobbie and Hazel had been to England before, although Bobbie had been too young to remember it. After they were married, Lucian Faithfull had promised his wife that he would take her to England if he ever got eighteen pence a pound for his wool. It was a pleasant prospect, and an unlikely one.

But to his surprise he actually did receive that vast amount, and it coincided with a minor dispute that had arisen between his sisters, one of whom was in England, over the maintenance of the big house at Springfield. So by going to England he could now keep his promise to his wife and settle the dispute at the same time.

They had left in 1901 and were away for nearly a year. They took with them the wife of one of the gardeners, an English woman who had been a nurse before she married. She had always looked forward to returning to England but had never thought it would be possible. Indeed, in the two years she had been at Springfield she had never once been into Goulburn.

The trip had been a great success, even though Lucian was an unenthusiastic traveller. But he had managed to resolve the dispute between his sisters and he had enjoyed the trip because of the pleasure it gave his wife. Unfortunately when they returned to Springfield in 1902 they found it gripped by one of the worse droughts on record, but that was one of the hazards of living on the land.

Nobody thought of such things now as they bustled around for weeks in a fever of preparation. There was so much to do and so little time in which to do it. Letters had to be written and instructions given for every possible eventuality. Springfield must continue to function as an efficient sheep station even though its owner would be away for such a long time.

For the girls, preparing for the trip consisted of endless decisions about what they should take. Would this dress look dowdy and out of date in London? Would that be available once they left Australia? For Bobbie, then fourteen years old, it was a very serious matter.

Her mother solved one problem, at least. Knowing that they would be at sea for six weeks, and knowing that it was almost impossible

to get washing done even on a luxury liner, she took the older girls into Goulburn and bought an enormous number of dark muslin dresses which were 'practical'. They were awful too, but that did nothing to reduce the excitement.

The big house at Springfield when Bobbie was a young girl.

They joined the ship in Sydney and it sailed with the traditional send-off of streamers, flags and the throaty sirens of nearby ships that quite drowned out the cheering of the crowds on the wharf. Tugs and ferries scurried around and sounded their whistles as the liner made its way slowly down the magnificent harbour towards the heads. Any passenger ship 'going home' deserved, and received, a send-off such as that.

As the ship made its way south everybody tried to settle in to the conventions of shipboard life. It was, for example, incorrect to dress for dinner on the first night out, but essential to do so after that. Acquaintances were made, but only tentatively at first. It would be a long journey and it would seem even longer if one could not get away from the bores, the prattlers, and the social climbers.

17

The girls, of course, cared nothing for such things. Valerie was only nine and still in the care of a nurse, so she took little part in the activities of the other two. But for Bobbie and Hazel it was a whole new world and they examined every part of it with wonder.

One thing that was new was that all the menus were in French, and, as far as they were concerned, not very informative. Their mother explained as best she could and the girls then pointed to the item on the menu so the waiter would know what to bring. It was, of course, more difficult when they were alone. Then Bobby found herself spluttering in embarrassment as she asked for a strange dessert she called 'blank mange' and which sounded to her like something a horse might go down with. She was even more embarrassed when the waiter called it blancmange. She knew what that was, but she had never seen it written before.

But before long they had settled into a routine that was extremely pleasant. There were deck games during the day and competitions of all kinds. They noticed that one girl seemed to have an endless supply of dresses that were just right for these activities, in contrast to their own dark muslin, but it was of little concern.

If the days were enjoyable, the evenings were even better, for there was dancing. They had both learnt to dance at classes in Goulburn, but they had seen little of the real thing. Now it was unlimited. It was, of course, formal too. When Bobbie wrote in her diary that she had enjoyed several dances with a very competent partner she referred to him as 'Mister X'. Mister X was fourteen too.

Her mother was remarkably trusting in all this. 'She never chaperoned us, which was very unusual then. She thought we would learn more by looking after ourselves, and she was quite right. One mother kept rushing on to the deck to see what her daughter was doing, so her daughter flirted away like mad knowing that she would soon be rescued. I was much more careful because I knew nobody was going to rescue me!' The only rule was that she had to say goodnight to her mother before she went to bed.

Although the ship was luxurious for that time, as it sailed west through the Indian Ocean it became a good deal less comfortable. There was no air conditioning and as the temperature increased the only relief came from constantly moving fans. Even in port the temperature on the ship was often far higher than that on the land.

One of those ports was Colombo, where the ship called to take on more coal. 'You had to have the porthole closed all the time and the whole ship got terribly hot. We watched the natives bring the coal on board and you cannot believe that people had to work like that. They ran up the gangplank with a sack of coal on their back, tipped it into the hold, then ran back down for another one. The whole ship was covered in coal dust, and so were we. Some people left the ship and spent the time in a local hotel. It was awful.'

The next stop was much more pleasant. The ship reached Suez at Easter and their parents had agreed that Hazel and Bobbie could go ashore with a younger couple and travel overland with them before rejoining the ship at Port Said.

'That was the most marvellous Easter. We spent two days in Cairo and went out to see the pyramids. There were donkeys and camels that you could ride so that you could see over the whole area. Actually there were only two camels, so this couple said Hazel and I should take those and they would ride the donkeys. We thought that was very good of them. But then we were very surprised because the two of them started chasing each other around the pyramids on their donkeys. Of course, our parents were much older and we had never seen them behave like that. In fact, until then we had never seen any adults really enjoying themselves. But they certainly did. They had a much better time than we did on the camels!'

From Port Said the ship sailed down the Mediterranean on the final stage of its long voyage to England. 'I think our parents were getting a little bored by then because the routine didn't alter much when you were at sea. My father was very good but I don't think he really enjoyed it. Mother said that she thought his greatest worry was that we would all be drowned at sea and he wouldn't be buried up on the hill at Springfield with all the other Faithfulls.'

Bobbie and Hazel were never bored. Being on the ship was like one big party which went on for day after day. But as they approached Plymouth they became more and more depressed, because they were to leave the ship there and the party would come to an end. But at least they would be in England.

They travelled up to London by train and as it puffed its way slowly through the western counties they watched the green English countryside roll past the window. Small, neat farms dotted with massive oaks and elm trees, tumbling rivers, trim villages dominated by spires and towers of ancient churches, and country lanes that ran between tall hedges of hawthorn. It was not at all like Springfield.

And on to London. 'I don't think young people would believe what London was like in 1914. There were hardly any tourists then. When we went to Westminster Abbey there were just a few quiet people looking around. Now, there are so many people you would think it was the Sydney Show.' There were motor buses, large and red and covered with advertisements, and they clambered up the narrow, twisting staircase to sit on the open top deck. Everybody said that you had the best view of London from there.

In contrast to the harsh Australian sun, Bobbie thought the softer, mistier light of London quite magical. 'We walked down Fleet Street and then up Ludgate Hill to St Pauls. It was in the afternoon and the sun was on the front of the cathedral. We first saw it as we walked down Fleet Street, so it was still about a mile away. I didn't take much notice of the streets because they were dominated by this huge sunlit building on top of the hill. I've seen it many times since, but I'll never forget the thrill of seeing it for the first time in 1914.'

There had been many changes since the parents' visit in 1901. There had been no motor buses then and the horse-drawn buses and hansom cabs that had been so common had now all but disappeared. They found one hansom cab, but that was in the South Kensington Museum and it amused her mother to think that things had changed so quickly. But it didn't surprise Bobbie. Anything that old deserved to be in a museum.

They visited relatives, were shown London by their cousins, and went by train to Scotland. Then, leaving Valerie and her nurse at Bournemouth, they steamed across the English Channel to explore the Continent.

They spent part of June in Paris, staying at the Hotel St Petersbourg which boasted that it had steam heating and a lift. On 22 June Bobbie wrote a dutiful letter to Aunt Flory, far away at Springfield.

'Today mother, Hazel and I went to the Louvre for the third time. Daddy is sick of it. And this afternoon we went to look at the shops, they have the prettiest hats. Most of the shops seem to be either hat or jewelry shops. The sales are on now and the big shops have tables outside with the goods piled on top. At the hat table there is a looking

glass and everyone trying on hats out in the street. On Thursday we are going on to Switzerland. The train starts at quarter past eight and we arrive in Lucerne at six o'clock, a very long journey but all the country will be interesting I expect.'

Bobbie, right, and Hazel in England in 1901.

Six days later the heir to the Austrian throne was murdered at Sarajevo, but it did not seem important.

Their time in Switzerland was all they hoped it might be. They were overwhelmed by the scenery and became almost giddy on it. Then Lucian Faithfull introduced a new rule. Wherever they stayed, they were allowed to go up only one mountain. This hit Hazel very hard as she had been looking forward to a second expedition from Lucerne before this restriction was announced.

They did, however, take the tiny train from Interlaken which wound its way up an Alpine valley and crept past the foot of the north face of the Eiger to arrive, hot and steaming, at the village of Grindelwald. From there they were taken to the top of Jungfrau, one of the highest mountains in Switzerland and which, on a clear day such as this, offered a view that seemed to stretch to the end of the world.

The family returned to London at the end of July. Bobbie had made herself useful to her father by willingly running errands for him, and because of this there had been little talk of sending her to school. And she also knew a little more about him now. When they had reached England he had given Bobbie and Hazel £10 each as spending money. Realising how carefully her father controlled his own money, Bobbie set out to do the same and meticulously recorded everything she spent.

Now they were back in England their father suggested that they probably needed more money by now, and asked them to account for the original £10. 'I must have been an awful prig, really. There I was with my account, all added up, and he gave me another £10. But Hazel had not been as thorough as I had and she had a dreadful time trying to remember everything. She got to within a pound or two and I told her to make something up, but she said she couldn't do that. He gave her the money, of course, but he gave her a long lecture as well. He was a generous man, but he didn't like you to think you could go to him and get £10 whenever you felt like it.'

So far they had travelled everywhere by train and had spent several days in each place. Now, Lucian hired a car so that they could spend a day exploring part of the West Country before returning to Valerie and her nurse at Bournemouth. Part of that day was spent in the Doon Valley.

'Before we left home my governess let me read books about England instead of doing normal lessons, so I knew a lot about these places because of that. I remember when we were going to Kenilworth Castle my knees were shaking with excitement, to think that I was really going to see it. I don't suppose people read those books now, but Scott and Dickens and the others were part of my life then.'

The Doon Valley was, if anything, even more thrilling than Kenilworth Castle.

'We stopped at the Lorna Doon Farm and we hired little Exmoor ponies that we rode about. We thought that was marvellous, riding over the moors and along the valley. But it is very exaggerated in the story because you could ride the horses down the side of the valley quite easily.' Or you could if you had learnt to ride before you could walk.

For Bobbie Faithfull, that English summer's day was spent in the company of Lorna Doon. But for others it was memorable for a different reason. It was 4 August 1914, and on that day Britain declared war on Germany. That apparently insignificant murder at Sarajevo was about to change the face of Europe.

Two-year-old Bobbie, in England in 1901.

'I don't remember thinking about a war or even hearing about it before then. I don't know whether my father did. I suppose he must have known what was happening, but it seems extraordinary that we were in Europe only a week or so before it started. Even when it broke out nobody seemed to really believe it. It was all going to be over by Christmas, anyway.'

There were soldiers camped not far from Bournemouth. 'They were tiny men, mostly from the Midlands, and many of them had never seen the sea before. They used to rush down to the beach in such excitement and stand looking at the ocean.'

23

The soldiers, caught up in a patriotic fervour, put on concerts for the equally patriotic civilians. Together they sang of a British supremacy that nobody could possibly doubt.

'Whenever I hear *Land of Hope and Glory* now I always think of that time. I loved singing and I joined in with great enthusiasm. Everybody sang, "Wider still and wider shall thy bounds be set", and it was all very emotional. You didn't think that those bounds could only get wider if other people's got smaller, and that it mightn't be so pleasant for them.'

In spite of the enthusiasm and the confidence, Lucian Faithfull realised the folly of staying in Britain. The trip would have to be cut short and they should now return to Australia as quickly as they could.

It was not an easy thing to do. Many people wished to leave Britain at that time because the chances of being able to do so in a few months' time were very uncertain. Shipping companies were rushed as people clamoured for berths on the few services which continued to operate.

Lucian Faithfull was fortunate. Early in 1915 he and his family boarded a liner for the return journey to Australia. As the ship made its way down the English Channel the weather was so foul that the captain was barely able to leave the bridge. They were in a small cabin in the bow of the ship and every time it hit a wave there was a loud crash and the whole of the ship seemed to twist and shudder.

'There was a woman in the cabin opposite who kept screaming so much that they had to get the doctor to her. I couldn't understand it because I thought it was terribly exciting. We would all take to the boats and I would help the women and children and it would all be very dramatic. Strange what you think as a child. I would be terrified now!'

4

School at Last

W_{HEN THEY} were safely back at Springfield Bobbie, who was now
fifteen and who had so far been educated entirely by governesses, knew
that it would not be long before she was sent away to school. It was
not an attractive idea. Springfield had open spaces and horses and
freedom, and even a governess could be diverted fairly easily.

It was not that she resisted education, indeed considering the
little she had had she was remarkably well informed. It was the strict-
ness, the rigidity of it that made it unattractive. At Springfield she
was 'Miss Florence' and most of her time was her own. She knew it
would not be like that at school.

Shortly after their return, then, Bobbie Faithfull was sent to
school in Sydney. It was an exclusive ladies' seminary run by Miss
Conolly and it occupied a large two-storeyed building in a leafy street
in Point Piper, an expensive suburb on the shores of Sydney Harbour.
Called Westwood, Miss Conolly's seminary was joyless, very strict,
and totally unforgiving.

It was the first time Bobbie had been away from her family and
she was, as she says, 'very spoiled'. Now she had to live with girls who
were complete strangers and who, because they had been there longer,
knew more of the system and had been able to come to terms with
it. They knew the rules and had learnt how to get on with each other,
but for Bobbie it was a completely new and unpleasant world.

'My mother had bought me some white silk stockings when we were in London and I was supposed to wear these when I went out. But all the other girls had lysle stockings and they teased me and pinched my legs whenever I wore the silk ones. So I stopped wearing them. The first time mother came to take me out she asked me why I was wearing those awful lysle stockings and I told her how dreadful everybody was.'

Later she pinned a postcard of Switzerland above her bed and cried herself to sleep nearly every night. 'I used to wonder what I had done to deserve it.'

The teachers did not help, although in truth they may have been more aware than they seemed at the time. With Victorian thoroughness they set about to deflate this grazier's daughter and to introduce her to a world that she had been a long time meeting. And they did it with sarcasm and outraged indignation. 'I got into dreadful trouble once because two buttons on my nightdress were undone. Miss Conolly said she thought I was a girl she could trust!'

Even when Bobbie made a practice of taking two younger girls out for walks she was scorned — 'You are so careless you'll probably be the death of them'. And she had always assumed that if an adult wanted her to do something, they would ask. She had always responded readily and willingly, but that was not enough for Miss Conolly. It would be a very unpleasant person who would not do something they were asked to do, she said to Bobbie, but wouldn't it be much better if she thought instead? Then she would not have to be asked.

She had never faced such treatment before, and it made her miserable. It was as if she could do nothing right, as if the whole world took her for a fool.

'Then I remember thinking that I wasn't all that stupid. I knew I was behind in lessons because I had only had governesses and because of the time we had spent travelling, but I didn't think I was stupid. So I decided I would show them that I wasn't. It made me obstinate. I would not give in.'

Most of the boarders at Westwood were, like herself, from country families. Although a few were daughters of professional men, most were from the land and their fathers, like hers, were graziers. 'They all thought the place they lived on was the best place in Australia, and their horse was always the best horse. The size of the place didn't

At the Goulburn
cathedral fair in
1904.

matter, but it was always the best. They all came from families who
were important in their district, just as I did.'

Although she had much in common with them, in many ways
Bobbie Faithfull was much more sophisticated because of her travelling.
'It really had done me a great deal of good, even though a lot of what

I had learnt was no use here. But I had danced with a boy on a ship when I was fourteen, and none of them had done that!'

Miss Conolly, in charge of the daughters of some of the most respectable families in the state, thought any contact with boys was worse than an epidemic of measles, and both had to be avoided at all costs. One girl was caught talking over the fence to a boy who had once stayed with her family. She was sent to bed in disgrace.

The aim of Westwood was to teach girls to be ladies. It was about manners, respect, and the social niceties that would be essential in their future role as wives of gentlemen. Academically it was less distinguished than many schools, although two of Bobbie's friends did go on to university from there. 'That was very novel and it caused a great deal of discussion. Everybody thought it would be rather terrible and that they would meet all sorts of funny people there.' But Westwood had one advantage which Bobbie thought very enlightened. It did not sit for external exams.

They let her stay in a class for her age in arithmetic, which had recently been extended to include algebra as well, but she moved ahead in literature, history and geography when she showed that she could keep up with the older girls. She had not learnt those things so much as absorbed them. She had read widely before going to England and the history came with the stories. And travelling halfway around the world and back, and through part of Europe, had given her a knowledge of the world without much effort on her part.

One of the subjects taught at Westwood was carpentry, unusual for a girls' school now but quite common then and even highly regarded. Bobbie made a wooden box which she decorated with skilful carving on the top and the sides and which is still kept in the big house at Springfield. 'A few years ago a magazine reporter came to do a story about the place and she picked up this box and said what a wonderful antique it was. I was quite insulted! It might have been an antique to her, but I could still recognise the bits I hadn't got quite right and it didn't seem all that long ago.'

Westwood also had religion, and in great quantity. It was traditional Church of England and it was a constant background to the rest of the school's activities. There was a church service at school every day and on Sundays the girls were walked in a crocodile to All Saints at Woollahra. It seemed as if they spent a considerable amount

Visiting the Pyramids while en route to England in 1914. Hazel, left, and Bobbie on the camels, and their friends on the donkeys.

of time on their knees. Once, when she was accused of not cleaning the toes of her shoes, Bobbie said that they were worn away through praying.

Her attitude to religion was not one of enthusiasm. It was a convention which seemed harmless enough, but she was already sceptical of it. She did, however, have one of her prayers answered.

It was the custom for the school to give a concert at the end of each term. Parents arrived and listened to the girls as they sang, or played the piano, or did their best with violins that were usually too big for them. Although Bobbie had learnt to play the piano she was not good enough for a public engagement of that kind, much to her relief.

'Then one day I was busy playing Mendelssohn's *Hunting Song*, which I might say had taken me two years to learn, and I was going through it with great enthusiasm. Then Miss Conolly came in and said she didn't know I could play like that. "You can play that at the next concert," she said. I nearly had a fit. I couldn't see how I could get out of it, so I prayed every night for something to happen. And it worked. Miss Conolly fell ill just before the concert and it had to be cancelled. But praying has never worked for me since.'

The Doone Valley, Devon, which Bobbie and her family visited on the day the First World War broke out.

Bobbie's recollection of Westwood is incomplete, as if it were a part of her life that was, on the whole, so consistently unpleasant as to be not worth preserving. There was, for example, the time when it was announced that their evening meal would be simpler than in the past. Instead of having bread, butter and jam they would now have either butter or jam, but not both. The reason, Miss Conolly explained, was because of 'the poor Belgians'. 'We were all very scornful about that. We couldn't see how any Belgian was going to benefit because we didn't eat butter or jam.'

There was also the incident of the towel which taught her something of people, both old and young! Each week the girls had to hand in their towel so it could be washed. One day Bobbie forgot, and was terrified of the consequences. Her room mate gave her the solution. 'Go up to Miss Conolly,' she advised, 'and just give her the towel, saying that you forgot to hand it in.' Nonchalance, it seems, was the key.

It was a terrifying prospect, but Bobbie decided to give it a try. And it worked. Miss Conolly took the towel and told her not to do it again, just as a much younger girl arrived with her towel. 'She was a poor, frightened thing and she kept saying how sorry she was. Miss Conolly was very nasty to her and told her that she would have to keep it for another week for being so stupid. People's characters are extraordinary, aren't they?'

When she had just turned seventeen, Bobbie returned to Springfield at Christmas believing she had left Westwood forever. But the girls had prepared a petition which they sent to Bobbie's mother, urging her to send Bobbie back for another few months when the new term started. Rather to her own surprise, Bobbie was glad to return. She no longer had the terror she had had when she was fifteen, and she had long since stopped believing she was stupid.

There were some surprises. First she was made one of the head girls, and then Miss Conolly asked her mother for permission to take Bobbie with her on a trip to Tasmania. Already a keen traveller, Bobbie would have gone with the Devil himself.

Hazel and Miss Conolly's mother made up the party, but they found the first part of the trip, the sea crossing, most uncomfortable. The sea was rough and most of them were seasick all the way across. Bobbie, on the other hand, walked around the deck and fell into conversation with a man who was one of the few other people about.

The result later was a stern lecture for talking to a man before being introduced to him. 'Even then I thought that was ridiculous. And it became even more embarrassing later. We went on a coach trip round Mount Wellington and he was on the same trip. I hardly bared my teeth at him. I thought that if I said anything to him Miss Conolly would send me home and I didn't want that. I would go anywhere with anyone to see something new.'

In the middle of the year, when she was seventeen and a half, Bobbie Faithfull left Westwood for the last time and returned to Springfield.

'Although I certainly didn't like it, I think that school did me a lot of good. Sooner or later you need to accept that other people do not think of you in the way your family does. I learnt that at school, and it was better to learn it there rather than later. I was spoiled when I went to school, and they got rid of that. I once asked my mother years later why she had sent me to that school. She said, "I think it's a good thing I did because I don't know what you would have been like if you hadn't gone there".'

5

Back at Springfield

HAVING LEFT school in the middle of 1917 Bobbie Faithfull returned to live with her parents in the Cottage at Springfield.

Although the war was still raging in Europe, little had changed at Springfield because of it. It had brought personal grief, to be sure, for by then almost everybody had lost a friend or relative in that distant conflict. But apart from that the effect on this part of rural Australia was slight. Springfield was, after all, more attuned to the passing of Australian seasons than it was to the fury of war in Europe.

Springfield was still a village, though now slightly larger. In the centre of the main station area was a large open space which served as a village square. One side was occupied by the back of the big house, which was protected by a modest screen of trees and shrubs. This was the part of the house that was entered by station hands when they had need to, perhaps to carry in a supply of wood or when going into church.

It would have been unthinkable for them to have used the front door. That was reserved for members of the family or their guests. Sometimes it was a matter of fine judgment. The clergy, of course, enjoyed the privilege without question, but most ram buyers would have been uncertain about their rights, especially as there was a separate room for their use at the back of the house. Visiting tradesmen, on the other hand, had no doubt which entrance they should use.

The front door itself was on the narrow side of the house and gave on to the broad gravel drive which stretched away to the left to run down an avenue of tall trees before reaching the boundary of the garden. There, it joined a station road which ran to the main gate on the Goulburn road. To the right of the front door the drive ran a short distance to finish at a gate which opened on to a corner of the square.

The western side of the square consisted of a long, low bluestone building which contained the carpenter's workshop and several store rooms. Facing it across the square was the coach house, a large brick building which looked almost like a church. It housed the coach that Brewsters had built and which was still used by Aunt Flory. But soon even she decided she should have a car, and after that the coach saw little use.

Next to the coach house was a small stable which William Pitt Faithfull had built in the 1850s, and alongside that was a newer building that Lucian had built for his motor car.

The fourth side of the square, which faced the back of the big house, was dominated by a huge barn which had a double-storey gable in the centre. This was the old mill and it had been built by William Pitt in the early days of Springfield. The building and machinery were masterpieces of bush craftsmanship. They had been built by a man who had once been a ship's carpenter and, using the most primitive of tools, he had erected a substantial timber frame using rough logs that Springfield offered in abundance. He had then fashioned the milling gear, making huge cogged wheels whose timber teeth meshed perfectly with those of their neighbour. A horse was used to turn the main shaft. It walked patiently in a circle while the machinery above creaked musically as it ground flour from the wheat and sent it down a chute of polished wood to be collected in a sack at the bottom.

The mill had not been used for a long time but it was still complete and Lucian Faithfull claimed that it would take no more than twenty-four hours to bring it back into service. Not many on the place agreed with him, but all were aware that he had a great affection for the old building and the machinery it contained. He had, indeed, replaced the wall shingles with corrugated iron and although this made the building less attractive it had certainly helped to preserve it.

Behind the mill a complete street ran down the slope of a paddock towards the river. The street contained several houses that were used by staff and some of these houses, towards the end of the row, looked across the paddock to the earliest part of the big house. At the bottom of the street were the shearers' quarters and not far from them stood the small slab hut which was the Springfield school, soon to be replaced by a newer building on the other side of the square.

Behind the coach house, near the gate that led to the big house, stood the woolshed. It was built of brick and because of its coolness it was regarded by shearers as a 'top shed'.

And beyond the yards that surrounded the shed stood the Cottage, large and rambling and comfortable, and the home once more of Bobbie Faithfull.

The life that she returned to was as comfortable as she had known as a child. It was a life of pleasure and leisure and her responsibilities were no greater than they had been then. She still rode as much as before, she played tennis, she read, and she visited friends.

These were mostly girls she had known at school and she never turned down an invitation to stay with them. 'I loved seeing different places. That was the main reason. By that time I had lots of friends and whenever anybody asked me to visit them I always went.'

Important though these visits were, and the return visits which they led to, they were never very frequent. 'People simply did not move around in the way they do now. Graziers and other landowners might meet at the Sydney Show, but apart from that they hardly ever saw each other from one year to the next. If they were keen on racing they would usually go up to Sydney for the Spring Carnival every year, and others might meet socially at the polo. But they really were quite insular and everybody pretty well kept to themselves. There never was anything like a sheep-breeders club, you know, where they could get together and run the country. They just concentrated on running their own place.'

Most of the running of Springfield was in the hands of the gentleman manager, Mr Harris, who had ridden for the doctor in Goulburn the day Bobbie was born. He now lived with his family in a house at Pinea, where Lucian Faithfull had originally hoped to live. Mr Harris was in charge of the men and directed them in accordance with Lucian's instructions. Lucian continued to class the sheep and Bobbie rode

around the paddocks with him and learned about the finer points of
sheep breeding. 'The rams had to have a soft nose and straight backs.
He was a very fine judge of sheep in that traditional style but it was
embarrassing sometimes when I went to the shows with him. He used
to show me where the wool had been left a little longer on the sheep's
back to make it look straighter than it really was. He had given up
showing by then, but he always said he never did anything like that!'

Breakfast in the big house.

The times Bobbie and her father spent looking at sheep or talking
about them were the closest they spent together. 'At that time my
sisters were not as interested in sheep as I was. So I would go with
him and he seemed to enjoy telling me about them. I learnt a lot that
way.'

Bobbie was more mobile than most girls in those days because
she already knew how to drive. 'My father taught me on the car he
had then, which was a BSA. He had met a man in his club who said
that his daughter could drive and she was only fifteen. I was only

35

twelve at that time, but my father came home and announced that he was going to teach me to drive.'

There were few legal complications. All that was needed was a licensed driver, and in their care a learner could take to the road immediately. Bobbie's first lessons were held on the station roads, but before long her father had her driving along the main road to Tarago, a small settlement on the way to Braidwood. It was a terrifying experience for while Bobbie tried to keep the car on the narrow road, her father rested his gun on the back of her seat and shot rabbits in the paddocks as they drove past.

The BSA was fairly easy to drive but, like all cars at that time, there was no synchromesh on the gear box and this raised gear changing to something approaching an art, especially when changing down. First you took your foot off the accelerator, then you pressed the clutch and moved the gear lever into neutral. You then released the clutch and at the same time used the accelerator to increase the speed of the engine so that the gears that were about to come together were moving at the same speed. You then pressed the clutch again, moved the lever into the lower gear and accelerated away.

If you did all this well, the gear was changed smoothly and the car continued without hesitation. If you did it badly, the car lurched violently as the engine adjusted itself to the new speed. And if you did it abominably the car stalled with a screech of protesting cogs which, in extreme cases, could finish up on the road.

Changing gear was even more difficult if you were braking as well, for then you had to use all three pedals in rapid succession. And if you were going uphill and missed your gear the car would start to roll backwards and there was then no alternative but to put the brake on and start again.

It was so difficult that many drivers at that time preferred not to change gears at all unless this was clearly unavoidable. Others enjoyed mastering it and were so proud of their skill that they did it on every possible occasion.

Lucian Faithfull came somewhere in between. He was not a good driver, but he was never a dangerous one either. Nor was he a particularly good teacher. He used to say that you should not depend on your brakes. When you were coming to a gate, he said, you had to steady up and let the car stop naturally. But Bobbie watched him and saw that he always sneaked his brakes on at the last minute, and so she did the same.

Hazel, on the other hand, was not so diplomatic. Carrying out his instructions to the letter she finished up ramming the gate and then protested that he couldn't do it properly himself. She was promptly demoted and handed over to the chauffeur for the remainder of her instruction. Not that the chauffeur was all that good either. He had been sent to Melbourne for training and on his return to Springfield had hit the gate as he turned in from the road.

When Bobbie was eighteen she and Hazel went into Goulburn to take their tests to become licensed drivers. This consisted of driving up one side of the street and then down the other side and so back to the police station to collect their licences. Hazel drove the car back to Springfield as dashingly as ever. When the chauffeur advised her to slow down for a bend she told him that she was now a qualified driver who needed no such advice, and promptly collected a post at the side of the road.

It was unusual then for women to drive. 'Some girls could drive, but few older women ever learnt. When I was visiting other places I don't think I met one mother who could drive. I don't know whether it was because they did not want to learn or because their husbands didn't want them to have the freedom.' Her own mother never learnt to drive, although she did try. And even Bobbie's trips were rarely any further than Goulburn. It was many years before she drove to Sydney, 'and that was a very big turnout, I can tell you'.

Not long after she received her driving licence, Bobbie had a brief encounter with another form of travel that was even more novel. One day in 1918 she went into Goulburn with Hazel and Valerie and while they were in the public library a woman asked them if they were going flying. She might well have asked if they were going to the moon, so unlikely was it. Thinking the woman might be a little strange, they made polite noises and started edging away. No, the woman said, they really could. There was a man with an aeroplane just out of town and he was taking people up for rides.

When they were outside the library Bobbie and Hazel looked at each other and decided that they were going to fly.

They found the man and his aeroplane in a paddock not far from the racecourse. Yes, he said, he would take them up for five minutes

Bobbie, centre, at her fourth birthday party which she shared with a friend in the front row who was thirteen on the same day. All the boys in this photograph were killed in the First World War.

and it would cost them £10. Well, he thought, he might be able to give them a little more than five minutes. The problem was Valerie, who was much younger and didn't have any money. They tried to explain this to her, but when she burst into tears Hazel said that Valerie could fly with her and when they came back Bobbie would go up by herself.

'It was an open plane with two sets of wings and when I watched them bounce over the grass as they were taking off I thought how unfortunate it was that I would have to be the one who went home to tell them that they had crashed!'

Fortunately, they didn't. Safely back on the ground, Hazel and Valerie clambered out, flushed and excited, and Bobbie took their place. 'We flew all round Goulburn and out over some of the nearer properties. But we didn't go over Springfield because that would have taken too long even in a plane. It was very bouncy and very noisy, but I loved it.'

When they returned home it was a long time before anybody could believe that they had actually flown in an aeroplane. And then there were some words from their father because they had not been able to pay for it at the time. One of his rules with money was that you did not have anything that you could not pay for. Even something as unlikely as flying over Goulburn in 1918 was barely sufficient reason for breaking that rule.

After leaving school, Bobbie and Hazel received money in the form of an allowance which they had to manage themselves. The allowance was not a periodic gift from their father as pocket money. Instead, he bought a quantity of shares for them and their allowance was the dividend that these shares produced. As such, the amount could vary from time to time, but in Bobbie's case her shares in a sugar company usually produced about £100 a year.

She had to buy her own clothes out of this, and if she visited friends she had to pay the cost of travelling. In fact, it had to cover all her own purchases, whatever they might be. 'And you were never supposed to spend it all, although I think I usually did. I spent most of mine visiting friends because I would rather do that and go short on clothes. It is funny to think of what I did to go and see places which later on I saw frequently.'

On the other hand, she had to pay nothing for living at home, or for anything else that was part of Springfield. The motor car was always full of petrol, and anything a horse might need was sure to be found in one of the storerooms.

It was, by any standard, a comfortable life, and it was supported entirely by the sheep at Springfield. But others had failed where William Pitt and Lucian Faithfull had prospered. Running sheep was not a licence to print money. Sheep and the property itself had to be run skilfully, and money had to be kept in reserve for the bad times that were an inevitable part of rural Australia. For those less skilful and less prudent, prosperity remained a dream and they struggled on, or gave up, while others founded dynasties.

Certainly the Faithfulls owed much to the foresight of William Pitt in selecting this land in the first place. It was never marginal land in the way that much of inland Australia was, and running Springfield never had much in common with pioneering in Queensland, for example. But things could still go wrong. The land could be so overstocked to take advantage of good seasons that a few bad seasons would bring devastation, or money which was needed to maintain and improve the property could be spent on good living instead.

Lucian Faithfull did none of that and his children grew up in comfort. But not, he thought, in extravagance. 'My father didn't seem to be affected much by droughts and he never got carried away by extremes. I don't think he was ever really pressed for money, but he never spent much and he was always very anxious that we shouldn't throw our money about.'

This was, of course, all relative. In the circles he moved in, he was not regarded as a flamboyant character; he maintained a standard that was appropriate to those circles but this standard was certainly beyond the means of most Australians at that time. Bobbie, too, accepted the comfortable life almost without thought. She had, after all, known no other and most of her friends, even those at school, had come from a similar background.

But she did know that others were not so fortunate. 'I knew that the people on the place did not enjoy the sort of life we had. I think I imagined they were different somehow, and I suppose they thought we were different too. I remember an old maid who was with us for years once said, "Let me do that, Miss Florence. You're not meant to be doing it".'

But the privilege also carried a responsibility. The people working at Springfield were part of the place. Many spent their working life there and it was their home just as much as it was the Faithfulls'. And they remained employed even if wool prices fell or if drought meant that stock had to be reduced.

'My father always had more men than he really needed because he never put anybody off. And if one of the men had a son who couldn't find work in the district he would put him on as a gardener until something turned up. Half the time the men were sitting round the stable doing nothing — not because they were lazy but because there were so many of them to do the work. But if he went out and roared they all sprang up and rushed about doing things, you know. I suppose on the wages they were paid you could afford to keep people on, but it was a very feudal turnout in many ways.'

Bobbie was more aware than most of the inequality, even though those on the wrong end of it usually accepted it philosophically. She

was, for example, appalled by the kitchen in the big house and the amount of work it caused Aunt Flory's staff. It was a very big kitchen, about thirty metres long, and it had a wood stove in one corner. The nearest sink was in the scullery next door and the cook had to walk the full length of the kitchen and then the full length of the scullery in order to reach it. She used to stand a jug of water on a table in the kitchen so that she did not have to make the journey too often.

A garden party at Springfield in 1904. Bobbie is sitting on her father's knee.

The kitchen itself had a flagged floor, although Aunt Flory had that taken up later and replaced it with lino, which she thought was very modern. It was also a long way from her dining room and her meals had to be carried along a covered verandah at the back of the house which was about fifty metres long.

The single men took all their meals in the kitchen and the maids took their meals in a separate dining room. 'It had one long table and the maids sat on benches down each side. There really was nowhere comfortable for them to sit, which I thought was awful. But at least they were warm and well fed. I do hope they were.'

Comfort meant different things to different people, but even some of the comforts enjoyed by the family would seem far from comfortable now.

Until 1914 the Cottage relied entirely on gas lamps for lighting. Then, just before the trip to Europe, Lucian installed electricity. There was, of course, no mains service to Springfield at that time and the electricity they used was produced by a petrol engine outside the house. 'The engine used to start up when you switched on the lights. It was very noisy but you didn't notice it much during the evening because it was running all the time. But if you went to the bathroom during the night and switched on the light, the engine would start up again and wake everybody up. There was not much privacy.'

Indeed, the system was capable of running lights and nothing else, not even an iron. Even the refrigerators continued to use kerosene. But being able to turn on a light was comfort of a high order, for previously anyone entering a dark room had to find matches and light one of the gas lamps. Her mother thought electric light was one of the blessings of the age and refused to have shades over the globes so that she might have as much light as possible. Lucian, on the other hand, thought it far too bright and insisted on wearing his broad brimmed hat in the house during the evening.

Aunt Flory thought electricity was dangerous and refused to have it in the big house. Instead, there was a large carbide gas plant in the garden next to the summer house, and the gas this produced was used to light the part of the house she used. The rest of the house continued to rely on lamps or candles.

Nor were there any torches, so that even though the houses might be lit, anybody going out after dark had to carry a lantern. If men were working outside at night they had hurricane lamps that used kerosene, but for shorter journeys a candle lantern was sufficient.

Water could not be heated by electricity or gas, and for many years a wood fire burning beneath a copper was used. When the Cottage was first built there was a copper in the main bathroom. The maid lit the fire underneath it and when the water was hot enough, which could take an hour or more, she baled it into the bath. Later, a boiler was installed in the maids' bathroom and the hot water was piped through the house, but it still depended on a wood fire.

There were wash stands in the bedrooms and in the evening the maid would stand a jug of hot water in each room. This was always rain water because nobody was expected to wash in the river water that supplied all their other needs. The maid would also put a towel over the jug to keep it warm and water and towel would be used before dressing for dinner. They always dressed for dinner.

Even when comfort was possible, nobody seems to have thought much about it. When the telephone came to the big house, for example, it could have been placed almost anywhere. In fact, it was installed in a small box which stood on the verandah at the back of the house. For the rest of Aunt Flory's lifetime she had to go out on to the verandah if she wished to use the phone. Day, night, hot or cold or wet, it was all the same.

'It was a curious mixture. I mean, we had so much comfort because we had a staff and you had all those things done for you, but you had so much discomfort as well. Like going to bed along an open verandah in the winter. But my father always thought we were very pampered. There were two gates on the drive from the Cottage to the main road and he used to say that we would soon be too lazy to get out and open them!'

6

Travelling Again

ALTHOUGH BOBBIE used much of her allowance to visit friends who lived on country properties, her love of travel could not be satisfied that easily. She had therefore continued to put money on one side so that she and Hazel could one day make a trip together.

It was a long time before they thought they had enough, for sums of that size were not easy to acquire. But in 1919, when Bobbie was nineteen years old, they thought they were ready. They had each saved £30 and they announced that they intended to go to Java.

Why Java? 'Well, we had seen England and much of Europe and the Middle East when we went in 1914, and anyway we knew we could not afford to go that far on what we had saved. So we thought we would like to see something of Asia. It was closer, and we knew it would be very different to anything we had seen so far.'

If most Australians at that time still thought of England as 'home', very few of them thought of Asia at all. And if they did, even fewer thought of going there. It was a perilous place, this teeming world of Conrad's stories. The people spoke strange languages, they had strange religions and their culture had little in common with almost anybody else's. In addition, their largely unwelcome appearance in large numbers during the Australian gold rushes had left an unpleasant legacy that lingered still.

Although most countries of south-east Asia were colonies of European countries, the Europeans who settled in them were thought to be a hardy breed. They had to endure a climate that was positively unhealthy and they had to administer a population that outnumbered them many times and who, for the most part, resented their presence. Only the adventurous went there.

And that reason alone was good enough for Bobbie and Hazel.

It is difficult to imagine what Lucian Faithfull thought of this proposal, but the fact remains that he agreed to it. Perhaps he assumed that his daughters would rarely leave the ship and would do little more than cruise around a few distant islands. Even so, they clearly could not go alone. They would need a chaperone. He selected a governess whom he thought would be very suitable. She would protect his girls from ship-board paramours and all the teeming hoards of Asia. She was twenty-six.

The three women joined a small ship in Sydney for the voyage to Batavia, now Jakarta, on the strange island of Java. It was not a boring journey. On board were a number of Dutchmen returning from holidays in Australia, a few adventurous Australian travellers, and a group of actresses who were making their way to Singapore.

There were parties every night and Bobbie was always asked to join in. They were wild affairs. Indeed, it was rumoured afterwards that the captain lost his ticket after his next trip for being drunk on the bridge, but as far as Bobbie was concerned he could not have been nicer.

She was looked after by a man who was about ten years older than she was, and she enjoyed his mature attention even though it verged on the paternal. Every night, when the party showed signs of becoming even wilder, he would escort her to her cabin door and say goodnight. 'I think in those days if you were really young and innocent people were very nice to you. All the men looked after us and fussed over us, but there was always a time to leave. Heaven only knows what used to happen after that!'

One of the passengers, a single man who was half Dutch and half French, was returning to the plantation he managed on the neighbouring island of Sumatra. He suggested that if they could make their way there he would be happy to show them something of the island.

They could stay in the town of Medan and he would collect them each day in his car and take them on excursions.

It was too good an offer to turn down. They had not intended to go to Sumatra but now it seemed a very attractive idea. They found they could get there by ship from Singapore, and they could return there for the start of the homeward trip. But not on £30. So when they arrived at Batavia the first thing they did was to send a cable to their father asking him to lend them £100, which they would repay from their allowances when they returned. It never occurred to them that their father might not approve of his daughters going to Sumatra. Perhaps it never occurred to him either, for he cabled the money by return.

They hired a car in Batavia and spent several weeks exploring the island of Java. Unfortunately they had been joined by an Australian who had been on the ship and who was already known to be an excruciating bore. 'He was a dreadful man. I could not understand why he travelled at all because he was always comparing everything he saw to Australia. When we were motoring he would say, "If those rice fields were wheat fields, this could be Australia".'

Eventually they could stand him no longer. When they arrived to look at the famous temple of Borobudor they claimed to be so impressed with it that they intended to spend a week exploring it. It was too much for him and to their relief he left to make his own way back to Batavia. It was no less than they had intended, and the following day they continued their journey in peace.

But when they too returned to Batavia they were dismayed to find that he was on the same ship for the voyage to Singapore. And as they sailed into that impressive harbour he explained that if this was that and that was something else, it could even be Sydney Harbour.

After spending a few days in Singapore the women boarded another steamer for the short voyage across the Strait of Malacca to the small town of Medan on the east coast of Sumatra. The man who had invited them met them there, but he had some bad news. There was, it seems, no accommodation available in the town and there was no alternative but for him to take them out to his chalet on the plantation. Unfortunately his housekeeper had just left, but he would do his best to make their stay as comfortable as possible.

It took several hours to drive to his chalet, which was high in the hills that surrounded Lake Toba. When they got there the scenery was magnificent, but there was little else.

'He was very kind and said that he hoped his house could supply everything we wanted. Well, we found that the bathroom was under the house and we had do go down a ladder from our bedroom to get to it. There was a well in one corner and a bucket of cold water that you threw over yourself. So one day Hazel asked him if we could have some hot water instead. The next day we were both in the bathroom without a stitch on when the door from the yard burst open and this huge man came in carrying a tub of hot water. Luckily I was able to grab a bath towel, but Hazel had no more than a face flannel and jiggled about with it as best she could. The man walked up to her very solemnly, bowed, and put the tub at her feet and walked out. By that time I was roaring with laughter, but Hazel didn't think it at all funny!'

There was, for Bobbie at least, an even greater surprise a few days later. She had taken a number of walks with the planter and had enjoyed his knowledge of the bush, which was considerable, so that soon these walks were a regular routine. The chaperone had suggested that perhaps it was not a good idea to walk alone with him, but Bobbie thought she was being silly. He was, after all, almost forty she thought.

But one day during their walk he commented that she seemed to spend a great deal of time at night praying before she went to bed. Praying? No, she said, if she prayed at all it was a very brief matter. But, he insisted, she spent a great deal of time on her knees before a small table in the room, so surely she was praying? No, no, she said, she was simply writing up her diary.

The conversation might have gone no further than that, except that Bobbie suddenly realised the implication of his remarks. How, she asked him, did he know what they did in their bedroom? His answer was frank, matter of fact, and disarming. There was, he said, a peephole in the wall. Perhaps, he suggested, it would be better if she didn't tell the others.

It was not long before she thought so too. They were in very remote country and they were totally dependent on him taking them back to Medan to catch their ship. If there were a scene, the consequences might be very unpredictable.

'So I didn't tell them. The chaperone would have been absolutely shocked to death, but she always turned her back on us when she undressed, so I thought she was pretty safe. And Hazel always loved anything dramatic and so I thought I had better not tell her either because she was sure to have made a scene. Sometimes she would walk around the room with nothing on and I would say that perhaps it would be better if she didn't. "Why ever not?" she would say, "It's awfully hot." It was years later before I told either of them what had happened.'

And beyond that, nothing did happen. 'I must say that he never really made a pass at me. He used to tell me a few stories that I think I was supposed to be rather shocked at, but that was harmless. And if he wanted to look at us through his peephole that didn't worry me very much either. I suppose it gave him some amusement.'

When the time came he drove them down from the hills and they caught the steamer back to Singapore. 'The Dutchmen we met when we were travelling all said that they didn't know what our father was thinking of, letting us travel in those places on our own. But we

never gave it a thought. Even staying in that remote house with a man we had met only on a ship didn't seem all that unusual then.'

What did seem unusual was that when the ship from Sumatra was late arriving in Singapore, the steamer they were to join for the voyage back to Australia had delayed its departure to wait for them.

'I bet they wouldn't do that now.'

Lucian Faithfull with a new car for Aunt Flory, with Valerie in the back. The car is a Minerva and was made in Belgium.

7

The Terranna Ball

As far as Bobbie Faithfull was concerned there was nothing, absolutely nothing, in the whole of the year as important as the Terranna Ball. It was the highlight of the social calendar in Goulburn and even people in Sydney were always glad of an invitation. It was sparkling, frequently noisy, and always exclusive. The rich were at play.

Terranna was much more than a ball, at least for most people. Terranna was a picnic race club and once a year, in January, it held a two-day race meeting at its course on the Gibson's property near the present village of Tirranaville. Membership of the club was a very high honour, the pinnacle of social achievement, and not many attained it. One journalist wrote, sourly but accurately, that you had little chance unless your ancestors had arrived with the First Fleet.

The Faithfulls had been founding members, along with the Gibsons, and their continuing importance in the club could not be denied. Most of the other members were also local landholders of importance, together with a few from the more honourable professions. But membership was strictly limited in numbers so that even those who were able to qualify might never get the chance.

Nor was there anything informal about the racing. Many people, including Lucian Faithfull, bred horses specifically to race at the Terranna meetings and their preparation during the weeks prior to the races was a matter of considerable importance. Some of the younger owners rode their horses themselves, for they were no strangers to galloping over rough ground, and horses would often compete in more than one race in a day.

This was racing as a sport, a rural sport in rural surroundings by people who knew about horses and liked to make them go as fast as they could. If you won, it was because your horse was the best on the day and you could take much pride in it. You could, indeed, talk about it for the whole of the following year.

As a picnic meeting for amateurs there was no prize money, and it would certainly have been out of place even if it had been allowed. Instead, the prizes were gifts that were donated by members. Old Mrs Gibson, for example, always gave a prize called the Bachelor's Bag, which supposedly contained all that a bachelor might need. And then there was the Lady's Bracelet. An owner would ask a lady if he could run his horse in this race on her behalf, and if he won he gave her the bracelet that he received as the prize. If your horse had little chance of winning, you could ask more than one lady provided they were unlikely to talk to each other.

In the members' enclosure, all the local properties built gunyahs of brushwood and erected a sign with the name of their property. They were meeting places to entertain other members and their guests whom they might not have seen since the previous meeting a year ago. Even though the meeting was held in the middle of the summer, dress was strictly formal. Ladies wore large hats and coloured chiffon, while the men wore formal suits, top hats, and carried silver-topped canes. It was as if the landed wealth of Goulburn was trying to recreate the splendour of Royal Ascot on turf that was kept short during the rest of the year by hundreds of grazing sheep.

Beyond the members' enclosure, the people of Goulburn and elsewhere had picnics on the grass.

The Terranna picnic race meeting had always ended with a ball. During the first few years this ball had been held in the ballroom of the Terranna homestead. But as its popularity grew, and as more and more people came as guests of members, it became necessary to move it to the Goulburn show ground. By then it was the society ball of Goulburn where eighteen-year-old daughters 'came out'.

'I missed all that, which was just as well because I thought it was ridiculous. Terranna was not held during the war years because the men were away and it didn't start again until 1920. Even though the war ended in 1918 it took much longer then to bring the men back to Australia. So the first Terranna Ball that I went to was in 1920, and as I was then twenty years old I didn't "come out". But it seemed a terrible idea to me anyway. When we were at school we could not even talk to a boy, but at eighteen we were supposed to be dressed up in white and have enthusiastic conversations with them.'

Hazel, on the other hand, was more disappointed, and more unlucky. She had wanted to come out before they went to England, when she was seventeen. But her mother said that she would have to wait. They would buy a dress for her in London and she would come out at the ball after they got back. 'But when we did get back the war was on and there was no Terranna. By the time it started again many of the boys she had known had either been killed in the war or had gone away and she thought she was too old, which was rather sad.'

By this time there were two balls during Terranna. On the Thursday evening there was a ball for those who were too young to come out, the young teenagers. The girls, who were not old enough to have their hair up, wore a large bow instead and were known as flappers. This ball finished fairly early, partly because of their age and partly because there was another day's racing on the Friday. The main ball, on the Friday evening, rarely finished before daylight.

'Everybody used to say that people met their future wives at the Terranna Ball. My father said he did. He said my mother was wearing a white dress with a blue sash and he said to himself that one day he would marry her. He told me that she was the only one he ever liked, and I was most impressed by that. But I found out later that he had already been engaged to a girl in Sydney and that he had broken it off.'

Preparations for the ball started weeks ahead. A new dress had to be bought, and that meant a trip to Sydney. 'The ones we thought were very smart had absolutely no chest. Your bra consisted of a straight piece of material that you buttoned tightly round you like a bandage so that it flattened you at the front. We thought anybody who was not absolutely flattened looked very dowdy.'

Bobbie, left, and Hazel, with their father.

And it had to be a new dress. One year, having spent all her allowance on travelling, Bobbie said that she would not be buying a new dress for Terranna that year. Her father, who had been reading his paper in the corner of the room, asked her if she really could not afford one and when she said she could not he broke all his own rules and told her he would pay for it. It was unthinkable that his daughter should go to Terranna wearing a dress that had been seen before.

The other part of the preparation was booking dances in the programme. This was issued a few weeks before the ball and listed the seventeen or eighteen dances that would be played during the evening. This programme, which had space for a name against each dance, was enclosed in a small folder and fixed to it by a silk tassel.

Once the programme had been issued, men asked the girls to book a dance for them. It was not a casual business. The men would ask personally if they could, but if not they would telephone or write a letter. Nor was it a casual business for the girls either. While they all liked to have a fully booked programme well before the ball, there was always the danger that they might then be asked for a dance by somebody they had just met, or by a favourite who happened to be late. Some might cut a dance with whoever had first booked it, but that was the height of bad manners and would not be forgotten. Others, more confident, would leave some dances unbooked for just such an event, but Bobbie never did. 'I didn't think I was enough of a belle to do that.'

During the Terranna weekend Bobbie and Hazel would have several house guests staying at the Cottage, most of them old school friends. After the last race on the Friday afternoon they would all return to Springfield to dress for the ball. Then they would have dinner with their parents before being driven into Goulburn by the chauffeur, who would stay there until they were ready to come home.

The ball started precisely at nine o'clock and it was held in the pavilion at the show ground which had been elaborately decorated for the occasion.

Surprisingly, perhaps, for such a glittering and important function, there was no orchestra. Instead, the music was provided by one man, a celebrated party pianist from Sydney called Mr Fay. He sat at an upright piano and with no assistance of any kind he provided the music for the entire night. 'Fay was the most magnificent pianist you could imagine for dance music. He could make you dance even if you didn't want to. He played one-steps and two-steps and so on, right through the programme. I could not imagine a Terranna Ball without Fay being there.'

After each dance the hall emptied as the younger people went outside and sat in cars. 'It seems curious now, but it was the thing to do then. You simply went and sat in the first car that had room. I remember one party we had at the Cottage. My mother and father thought they would look in to see if we were all enjoying ourselves and the place was deserted. We were all outside in the cars between dances.'

It was no less confusing to the parents and chaperones at Terranna. They sat around the floor inside the pavilion and occasionally even danced themselves — 'We used to think, "poor old things", but some of them couldn't have been more than forty' — but as soon as the dance ended their daughters disappeared into the night to God knows where. It made surveillance rather pointless as the only time it was possible was during a dance.

One reason for going out was so that the men could smoke or have a drink. Although there was a bar at the Terranna Ball, nobody would have thought of smoking in the hall. In fact, drinking was not as common as it is now and most girls didn't drink at all. 'When I had my twenty-first party at the Cottage, for example, mother provided a bowl of claret cup, and we all pretended to get giggly on that. But that was all. Oh, she did put in one bottle of whisky in case the old men would like a drink. But at Terranna I think the young men had spirit flasks in their cars. Especially those who had come back from the war.'

Much of the time was spent flirting in light-hearted and provocative conversation which, by convention, was not meant to be taken seriously. Bobbie found this confusing at first. 'I had been told that one man in particular always flirted with all the young girls, even though he was much older. So when I was having my dance with him he said to me, "You know, I only came here to dance with you". And before I could stop myself I said, "God forgive you for the lie!" I didn't want him to think I was so green that I believed him, but wasn't that silly? Now, I'd lap it up and pretend it was true!' Flirting was a skill and those who were good at it were invariably good company. Those who were less skilled could verge on the boorish.

There was, however, another convention that was far more serious, if only because it was more public. A girl had to be seen having every dance. A popular girl would have had a fully booked programme for weeks, others would have completed their programme during the races that day, while others might have filled their remaining dances during the early part of the ball itself. But for a girl to have a dance unbooked by the time it started was a public humiliation that few bore lightly, or, indeed, in public. Sitting with the old people at the edge of the dance floor only made matters worse, so a girl without a dance would invariably retreat to the cloakroom until it was over.

It never happened to Bobbie at Terranna, but it did once in Sydney. 'I had a friend from school days who was rather selfish and I had her down to stay when the polo was on. I remember we had to walk all round the polo ground because she couldn't see until she got next to a man she liked. Then I might as well have dropped dead, you know? Anyway, when I was staying with her in Sydney her family took us to a dance. Her mother was very nice and told this girl she had to look after me. But I didn't have one dance booked, and what was worse, this girl didn't introduce me to a single person. So I spent nearly the whole time in the cloakroom. That was a dreadful thing for a country girl in Sydney.'

One of the most important dances of the evening was the supper dance and the old people took great note of who was dancing with whom as it was supposed to be a sign of budding, if not actual, romance.

After that dance, everybody went in to supper and the pairing off then was no less significant. The meal itself was one of the highlights of the evening. Cold meats and desserts were laid out on each table and people sat where they wished, but usually with a group of friends and their partners. The meal was excellent, the flirting outrageous, and everyone looked forward to the second part of the evening.

After supper, the ball started to become more boisterous. Impromptu crocodiles would form up and Mr Fay would pound away as the crocodile wound its way around the hall or even threaded its way through the cars outside. Or the programme might be suspended while the men took over the floor for a rowdy game of touch football, or piggy-backed on each others' shoulders for a medieval joust.

During Bobbie's first ball in 1920 one of her cousins who had come back from the war even started dancing around with a gun in his hand. 'He came up to me and said he was going to shoot me and I just stood in front of him and told him to put it away. And do you know, he really did have bullets in the gun and a bit later somebody shot a couple of holes in the roof. I don't think it was him, but there was a terrible do over that and later on he had to face the committee and apologise.'

People started to drift away as the night grew older, but the diehards saw it through until dawn.

And when it was all over, people talked for weeks about the last Terranna Ball, and started looking forward to the next one.

During the twenties the formality of Terranna began to relax, but it was still as exclusive as ever. 'One year a woman from Sydney came to the races dressed in a simple linen suit and we all realised how much more sensible it was than yards of chiffon. And the ball too became more relaxed. People stood round the bar between dances instead of going outside.'

Terranna races and the Terranna Ball were held every year until the Depression in the 1930s made it inappropriate and both were abandoned. They were not mourned by most people in Goulburn, who resented the elitism of the members and all that the club stood for.

'I really do think they thought of themselves as the aristocracy. But they didn't seem to realise that the aristocracy everywhere was having a hard time by then.'

8

Manners and Society

A<small>S A YOUNG</small> woman, Bobbie Faithfull lived in a world where good manners were both highly regarded and almost universal. So much so that they were generally taken for granted, and only the lapses caused comment.

The emphasis was on consideration for other people and the belief that women deserved special attention, if not actual protection. They were the weaker sex, or so men thought, and because of that they were entitled to a unique kind of consideration.

This was so widely held that it cut across practically all social boundaries. Men wore hats and invariably raised them to women they knew even if they were doing no more than passing them in the street. Men stood up when women came into a room, they opened doors for them, they helped them on and off buses, and they carried things for them.

These were not just the manners of the city. Women in the bush were treated with the same degree of consideration, even though the men might be surprised and embarrassed that they were there at all. Mrs Aeneas Gunn described it well in *We of the Never-Never* when that book was first published in 1908, and it has not changed much since then. The changes have been greater elsewhere.

This code of conduct had some odd facets, or at least they seem odd now. Letters, for example, had a formality about them which was often quite out of keeping with their contents. When Richard Atkins wrote a letter to John Macarthur in 1796 accusing him of being a 'viper' and a 'monster of society', he signed the letter as 'Your obedient servant'. And if that was a long time ago, the formality of letter writing had lingered on. When William Pitt Faithfull wrote to his wife he signed himself, not Bill, not William, but W. P. Faithfull. And as young men, Lucian Faithfull and his brothers invariably signed letters with their full name even when writing to each other.

People would also address each other formally in a way that is hard to recall now. Bobbie automatically referred to her ship-board dancing partner as mister even though they were both young and she was safe in the privacy of her diary. Indeed, people might spend the whole of their working lives together and still be addressing each other as mister on the day they retired.

People in 'society' were, of course, supposed to have even better manners. But that wasn't always the case.

In 1920 the Prince of Wales, later to be King George VIII, carried out a tour of Australia that was triumphantly successful. Later that year Bobbie was invited to a ball held in his honour at Government House in Sydney. It was a young people's affair, with the guest list made up from others of similar families together with the naval officers who were accompanying the Prince. After the guests had all been presented to the Prince, an announcement was made. It was clearly impossible to introduce everybody to each other, so would people please feel free to dance with whoever might ask them.

It might even be the Prince, they said to each other, even though the thought terrified most of them. But it was more likely to be a naval officer, and so one of Bobbie's cousins explained to her that they lived on 'ships' which should never, ever, be called 'boats'.

'Sure enough, before long a grand, tall sailor came up and asked me to dance. I was wearing a long dress covered with silver lace that was very smart. It had things hanging down all over it and I felt quite confident. But when he swept me on to the floor I was suddenly petrified. He didn't say anything and so I thought I had better start a conversation. So I asked him what boat he was on. After that it got worse and worse. Then when we were in the middle of the dance

floor he suddenly said, "I'm very sorry, I hope you will excuse me, but I'm wanted". And he dropped me, or he thought he was going to drop me, in the middle of the floor. But unfortunately the buckle of his belt got caught up in my silver lace and as he walked away I was dragged behind. I let out an incoherent screech and he had to turn round and disentangle himself. Can you think of anything more embarrassing? I was only twenty and that was my first time at Government House.'

The chalet in Sumatra where Bobbie, her sister and their chaperone stayed in 1919.

Sixty-five years later, she was more charitable. 'I don't blame him. He must have thought he'd got an awful dud. I thought afterwards that it might have been Lord Louis Mountbatten, because he was out with the Prince. But I don't think he would have been so rude. At least he would have escorted me off the floor!'

If women generally were 'protected', those at Springfield were even more protected than most. Theirs was, after all, a very sheltered life and in any case the old attitudes survived longer in the country than they did in the cities. The first time Bobbie's mother saw a woman who had had too much to drink was on the ship going to England in 1914, and she was completely horrified. Indeed, she could hardly believe it, so alien was it. Bobbie herself did not have her first whisky until she was thirty, although her mother thought sherry was all right 'perhaps because it was more ladylike', and she did not smoke until she was over fifty. 'But I've made up for both since!'

Women were not supposed to be interested in business, for the men took care of that, and at Springfield there was a limit to what women could do. Hazel trained as a nurse, which was perfectly acceptable, and it was all right to work with children, but it was quite impossible to go out to work in the general sense.

'It really was a very sheltered background. I grew up knowing absolutely nothing.'

She certainly knew nothing of sex, for sex education was unheard of. 'Heavens, you didn't even mention the word sex. Those old teachers at school would have gone puce in the face. But I don't think we ever thought about it very much. Not like now. People seem to think they have just invented it, don't they?'

When she asked her mother why Oscar Wilde had been imprisoned (for homosexuality), she found that she didn't know either. She had asked her husband the same question and he had told her that she would not understand.

Bobbie believed, even when travelling with her sister and chaperone in Asia, that men would always behave properly. And, indeed, they did. She was full of confidence even though she knew nothing of such things. And when she was surrounded by people who were more enlightened, as she was on the ship to Java, she simply thought that they were somehow different. Not worse, just different. 'Nice girls didn't do that sort of thing. And nice men didn't take advantage of nice girls!'

But men could, of course, be autocratic. While Lucian Faithfull protected his family and provided them with the best, his word had the power of law if not the pomp. Nobody, he ruled, could go into Goulburn when the shearing was on, because the man who drove the car also looked after the machinery in the woolshed and it was important that he be there all the time. Nobody questioned his ruling and nobody went to Goulburn until the shearing was finished about three weeks later.

Bobbie willingly accepted the autocracy and the protection, albeit with some reservations. It was, after all, a pleasant way to be treated. If she were carrying a suitcase in Sydney it would not be long before a man, a stranger, would offer to carry it for her, and she would have no hesitation in letting him. Nor did she see anything wrong in a woman taking her husband's Christian name when she married. That was an honour.

Recently, she heard that a group of women had protested in a Goulburn hotel because they had not been allowed into the men's bar. They had said that they were quite good enough and could see no reason for the ban. But Bobbie thought they had got it wrong. To her, it was the other way round. The bar was not good enough for them.

'But I think men protected their women far too much. It was as if they put them on a pedestal and while that was quite nice, it was not very realistic, even then.'

Acceptance into this level of society depended on one thing above all: breeding. Nobody who knew it can pretend that classes did not exist in Australia. On the contrary, at this level they were as clearly defined as they were in England and in the old towns such as Goulburn and Bathurst perhaps even more so.

For a man to be accepted as an equal he had to be a gentleman, both by definition and by description. And if he was, his family would be accepted as equals too.

Gentlemen were well bred. They came from good families that had been visible for at least two generations, families that had always behaved with propriety and which could be relied on to do so in the future.

Owning land was not an automatic qualification, and certainly not in the first generation. People of all kinds could own land, often in vast quantities, but if they were uneducated and of unknown origin they were not regarded as gentlemen. If they were hard working and successful they would be admired for that, but it would need another generation before they could be considered as equal.

One could, of course, be a gentleman even if one did not have an acre to call one's own. Mr Harris, the manager of Springfield, was undoubtedly a gentleman. His children were also educated at West-wood instead of the Springfield school and he was universally respected

Mr Finley, schoolteacher at Springfield from about 1910 to about 1923.

throughout the district. If he was visiting a sheep property at nearby Crookwell, or selling sheep in Goulburn, he was acting with complete authority in the name of Springfield. He and his family were always invited to any functions held by the Faithfulls.

Most managers of properties enjoyed similar status. Indeed, a previous manager of Springfield had married one of William Pitt's daughters, and nobody thought that was unusual.

Some men were granted the honorary status of gentleman by virtue of their profession, even though their pedigree might be less than perfect. The local bank manager was always given this status, and so were clergymen. Other professions, such as medicine or law, were almost the exclusive preserve of those who were gentlemen in their own right.

Money was important only in the sense that it bought the right kind of education. It was that education, when combined with the correct breeding, that most accurately defined what a gentleman was.

Money alone was not enough, and might even be regarded with some suspicion. Being too friendly with people of that kind had its dangers even though one might have a genuine affection for them. 'My father always said that they would be sure to ask you for something. Well, not long afterwards I got to know this very nice family and spent quite a lot of time with them. But then they asked me if I would put them up for Terranna. It was very awkward because I knew they wouldn't get in at that time. I thought it was all very silly, but there was not much I could do about it.'

Surprisingly, perhaps, the lack of money in no way removed the status of gentleman once it had been attained. One of Bobbie's relations had little success in business and went droving in Queensland instead. On arriving at an outback property he would invariably be invited to stay in the homestead after a few minutes' conversation instead of being shown the usual quarters. He was a gentleman, and it showed.

One absolute disqualification in a country town was to be in trade. When Valerie was young she wanted to invite a girl from her dancing class to her birthday party. Her mother said she could not do so because she did not know her mother. Valerie asked, quite reasonably, if she could not get to know her. But that was not possible. They owned a shop. Even the wealthiest shop owner in Goulburn knew that there was no point in trying to become a member of Terranna, no matter how worthy they might be as local citizens.

Although part of this rigid system, Bobbie had a strong dislike of it even then.

'I thought it was ridiculous because everybody took it so seriously. Some people were determined to get on socially and I thought that was a very silly ambition. But if they succeeded you had to admire them for putting all that effort in. They must have had the go to get on, mustn't they? But I never could understand what was supposed to be so dreadful about running a shop.'

9
Marriage

IN 1921 THE THREE women who had travelled to Java and Sumatra decided to make one last trip together. It would be the last because Hazel was now engaged to a cousin whom she had met in 1914 and the older woman, who had been their chaperone on the previous trip, was engaged to a doctor who had recently returned from the war. Both were to be married within the next twelve months and there would then be no opportunity for them to travel together.

They agreed that this time they would go to New Guinea and in due course they went into Goulburn to make the booking. The clerk was very impressed and said they would be sure to have proposals of marriage somewhere along the way. They were very scornful and assured him that two of them were already engaged and the third, Bobbie, was not even thinking of such things.

The ship they joined in Sydney this time was small and miserable and offered neither charm nor comfort. They had booked a three-berth cabin which was by no means as large as they had expected. There were, indeed, only two berths that could justify that name. The third, they were told, was the day bed in the corner.

The other two were ready to abandon the trip as a disaster. There was not time to do so in Sydney, but they both agreed that they should all leave the ship when it reached Brisbane. But Bobbie did not agree.

It might be uncomfortable, but for someone who had endured the withering look of Miss Conolly in order to see Tasmania the prospect of seeing New Guinea more than justified a little hardship.

Bobbie told them that she would use the day bed if that meant that they didn't have to get off at Brisbane. It was agreed. It was also more uncomfortable than even she had expected. The weather was so cold that she slept with her clothes on and threw a coat on top of the bedclothes. When the bedclothes and the coat continually slid off the bed, she wrapped herself in a carpet and tried again.

When they reached Brisbane they were visited by an ancient aunt, who took one look at the ship and said she thought they were all quite mad. There was no doubt, she said even more sourly when she saw their cabin, that everybody took their pleasures in their own way. 'But I could put up with anything then, and I thought it was very exciting to be going to New Guinea.'

Nor did she have to put up with it for long. She had made friends with the purser and a few days later he gave her a cabin to herself which had been vacated by a passenger who had left the ship at Brisbane.

The ship eventually put in to Port Moresby and Rabaul and also called at Samarai, a small island off the eastern tip of New Guinea, before returning to Sydney. There were no invitations to exotic places this time, but Bobbie did receive a proposal.

'He was a man from Melbourne and he started to get quite serious. There was to be a fancy dress ball on the ship and I said I would go as an Aborigine called Topsy, who was a character in a book. But he wanted me to go as Frost and he bought up all the Epsom Salts in Port Moresby so I could sparkle. I thought that was a silly idea, so I took no notice and went as Topsy as I had intended. But he still proposed. I turned him down, I'm afraid, and he asked me not to tell anybody because it would make him feel silly. So of course I didn't. When we got back to Goulburn we were going past the travel office and Hazel said we ought to go in and tell the clerk he had been wrong. He hadn't been wrong at all, but I still didn't tell her!'

By this time Bobbie was not short of admirers, and romance was never far away. If not a belle, she certainly was good company. 'I think I was pretty easy. Oh, I shouldn't say that now, should I? It means something quite different. I used to say that we were all young and gay until my grandchildren told me I shouldn't say that either!'

After the trip to Java Bobbie had had some difficulty adjusting to the requirements of Australian society. 'When we were in Singapore there was dancing at the hotel and you were supposed to dance with anybody who asked you, even though you didn't know them. There were so few European girls there that the men would have only half the dance and then hand you over to somebody else. One man said, "I am sorry to be so dull but, you know, I don't often see girls". It quite spoiled me for when I came back to Sydney and I was supposed to entertain the man.'

Some of these admirers were invited to Springfield, but their visits were not usually very successful. 'My father never thought much of them, but I suppose he was like most fathers. I think most of them had no intention of being anything more than friendly with me. But if anybody even asked me out to a dance father thought they were after his daughter!'

As far as Lucian Faithfull was concerned, his daughter was overlooking the most eligible man he knew, and he kept telling her so. Bobbie reacted indignantly every time. Irwin Maple-Brown? She would not marry him, she said heatedly, if he was the last man on earth.

Irwin Maple-Brown was two years younger than Bobbie, which did little to help his cause. He had been born in South Australia and had moved into the Goulburn district as a child when his father bought the neighbouring property of Gundary Plains. As a boy he had ridden his pony into Goulburn every Saturday morning to attend the same dancing class as Bobbie, and had once told his mother that if Bobbie kept dragging him round the floor he would not go again.

Since that childhood trauma he had been educated at King's College in Goulburn, Tudor House in Moss Vale, and finally at King's School in Parramatta. After that he had worked as a jackeroo for the legendary Otway Falkiner, who owned the famous merino stud of Boonoke, near Deniliquin, and who was known as the 'Napoleon of the Old Man Plain'. Otway Falkiner had once said that Irwin Maple-Brown was the best jackeroo he ever had, and Falkiner's daughter later confirmed that he had meant what he said. Since leaving Boonoke Irwin Maple-Brown had been managing another property owned by his father called Cucumgilliga, which was near Cowra in New South Wales.

It is not surprising that Lucian Faithfull thought that Irwin was much more suitable than the men from Sydney. Lucian was then in his sixties, and the problem of who might run Springfield after his death was no closer to solution. His elder daughter had shown no interest in the prospect, and the man she was engaged to was set for different things. His younger daughter, Valerie, showed no inclination either. Bobbie was the only one who had learned anything of the place, and their closest moments had been when they were out together looking at sheep or when they were talking about them.

Bobbie was true to the bush. She had no wish to move to a city and her love for Springfield was obvious, whatever the future might bring. Lucian Faithfull simply wished the future to bring a man from the land. Having been denied a son, he looked for a son-in-law instead.

He must have been a patient man in his support for Irwin Maple-Brown, for Bobbie's scorn was the match of his enthusiasm. Not that Bobbie and Irwin had seen much of each other. He had been over to Springfield occasionally for polo practice and they met at social events such as Terranna as well. But as far as Bobbie was concerned he was no more than the young boy next door and she refused to take him seriously.

It was not that Irwin Maple-Brown was unattractive. On the contrary, he was a handsome man and already an outstanding polo player, and anybody with those advantages was never short of female company. It was simply because of his age that Bobbie could not consider him as a possible husband.

When the family's trip to England had been cut short by the outbreak of war, Lucian Faithfull had promised that if the war ever ended he would take them all to New Zealand to make up for their disappointment. He may well have forgotten this promise made, perhaps, in a rash moment. But Bobbie had not yet seen New Zealand, and it was time to remind him of it.

Lucian Faithfull was an even less enthusiastic traveller than he had been then, and he now rarely went much further than Goulburn. But a promise had to be honoured. It might also be a good idea, he said, if Irwin went with them. Bobbie thought it a dreadful idea and told Irwin that he had better bring his brother with him as well, otherwise he would have a very miserable time. So he did.

By the time they left they made a sizeable party. There was Lucian Faithfull and his wife, their three daughters, and Irwin Maple-Brown and his brother, 'and we all traipsed round New Zealand together. Can you imagine anybody doing that now?'

But if her father hoped to develop a romance between them, he was sorely disappointed. 'Irwin and I fought each other all the time. I remember once being very cross with him when we were on Mount Cook. We went for a walk together and I was looking at this beautiful mountain and everything, and all he could talk about was getting home to play polo.'

After they did return home, Irwin invited Bobbie to join his sister in a visit to Cucumgilliga. The sister was in truth a chaperone, no matter how unnecessary one seemed to be. Bobbie agreed to go, as she always had with invitations from schoolfriends, because she had not seen that part of the country before.

It was during that visit that her attitude began to change. She realised that Irwin Maple-Brown looked quite different when running a property. Until then she had thought of him only as a youngster, but now she saw him as a man doing a job that would have challenged somebody more than twice his age. He was trying to clear the place of rabbits.

Bobbie Faithfull knew a great deal about rabbits. When she was a child there had been so many on Springfield that at sunset it seemed as if the whole of the hillside was moving as countless thousands of them edged forward in their grazing. The men had netted them and poisoned them, and as each part of the property was cleared they had secured it against further invasion with rabbit-proof fencing.

But it was a much more difficult job at Cucumgilliga. The paddocks were not so open and there were huge boulders, some as big as a house, that gave the rabbits all the protection they needed. The previous manager had left in disgust and Irwin had then promised his father that he would succeed where the manager had failed.

Irwin was now working with thirty rabbiters, all of whom were older than him, and they needed a great deal of organisation. They needed supervision too, for it was generally thought that rabbiters would often deliberately leave a few rabbits behind in order to stay in work. Eliminating the rabbits completely was not, after all, in their best interest.

Bobbie was surprised at Irwin's maturity, for he had shown no sign of it elsewhere. And so Bobbie Faithfull, confident, well travelled and sophisticated and who had never missed a dance at the Terranna Ball, fell in love with the boy next door.

They were married in St Saviour's Cathedral in Goulburn on 9 October 1923 and it was the biggest wedding Goulburn had seen for years. It was an evening wedding, which was unusual then, and the streets around the cathedral were so crowded that the chauffeur had to struggle to get the bridal car through. Inside, the cathedral was crowded 'by a large and fashionable attendance' as Bobbie Faithfull, wearing a Paris gown of gold brocade moiré and a veil of Limerick lace, entered on the arm of her father. The organ played 'Oh, Holy

Spirit' as they made their way towards the chancel, followed by five bridesmaids, the chief of whom was Valerie dressed in an early Victorian frock of mauve morocain with gold chaplet and a mauve veil.

The ceremony was conducted by the Bishop of Goulburn, Dr Radford, and as the party retired to sign the register the organ played 'O, Father, all creating' as the congregation waited for them to reappear. A pause, some muted conversation, and then the organ burst triumphantly into the Bridal March from *Lohengrin* as the couple emerged and Irwin Maple-Brown led his wife down the long aisle towards the massive western door. There, they were greeted by a roar from the huge crowd gathered in the evening light so that at first even the bells of the cathedral could barely be heard.

The reception was held at the same pavilion in the show ground that was used for the Terranna Ball, but now hardly anybody recognised it. It had been decorated for the occasion by a lady from Sydney and its old interior had been transformed into a Persian rose garden. Huge rose bushes bloomed in each corner, roses climbed the walls and hung from the canopied ceiling and massive palms draped their fronds over the dance floor. In the supper room, rose-covered lattices and shading palms surrounded the tables, which were themselves strewn with pink and white sweet peas.

In one corner was a mountainous display of presents of all kinds. Among them was an oak and silver tray and service which had been given by the staff of Springfield to 'Miss Florence'. But she was Miss Florence no longer. Now she was Mrs Irwin Maple-Brown and those who had known her as Miss Florence were already calling her Mrs Irwin.

The Bishop presided, the usual toasts were drunk, telegrams were read, and then Berman's Jazz Band, which had been brought from Sydney, played for dancing. Later that night Mr and Mrs Irwin Maple-Brown left for their honeymoon in Melbourne.

They drove away in Irwin's car, an American Hudson which he had painted mauve because he knew it to be Bobbie's favourite colour. The first night was to be spent at Yass, and accommodation had been booked there. 'But when we arrived about one o'clock in the morning they said they hadn't any rooms. So they told us to go down to the Commercial Hotel — I often look at the old Commercial in Yass now — and there would be a slate with room numbers on it. If there was

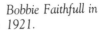

Bobbie Faithfull in 1921.

no name alongside a room we were to write our name and go in. It was a good thing there was one, otherwise we would have had to spend the night in the car.'

They spent the next night at Albury and then the following day they found the road to Melbourne was cut by a flood. 'Irwin was sure he could get through and he told me to keep pumping a lever that was on the dash board while he drove the car. I did that and then when we were right in the middle of this tremendous flood the car stopped and somebody had to pull us out with a horse. And then after that he had a race with another car and ours blew up. So instead of arriving at Menzies Hotel in Melbourne in a smart mauve Hudson, which I had been looking forward to, we turned up in a yellow taxi!'

When their car was repaired, they returned by the Princes Highway and spent a few days at Springfield before moving on again, this time to Cucumgilliga.

10

Cucumgilliga

THE PROPERTY of Cucumgilliga, which fronted on to the Boorowa River near Cowra, had little in common with Springfield.

By that time the Faithfulls had owned Springfield for nearly a hundred years. Every building, every fence, had a memory and there was history in almost every corner. It was also a famous property and was often referred to as one of the leading merino studs of Australia.

But hardly anybody knew of Cucumgilliga. It ran a commercial flock of sheep and depended almost entirely on the wool they produced. Nor did it have much history, for properties such as this, which made up the major part of the Australian wool industry, changed hands quite frequently. It was a work-a-day property that fought hard for a living. With none of the substance and prestige of Springfield, Cucumgilliga existed on a much sharper economy.

It was also even more isolated than Springfield. The country was wide and open and laid out with a seemingly endless succession of paddocks that ran for miles. This was good country and people did well there, but they had few comforts.

Bobbie moved into the modest weatherboard homestead and started her married life. 'I was very happy. At first I used to spend all day with Irwin, riding, cutting burrs, or doing whatever he was doing. There was always a great deal to do and not many people to do it, so I was able to make myself useful.'

The house was looked after by a cook and a housemaid, both of whom had come with her from Springfield. This was just as well, for Bobbie wasn't much of a cook and had never done much of it. There was one time when they didn't have a cook at the Cottage and Hazel had thought it would be nice if the two of them did it. They took it in turns for a week, but when their mother found a cook who was willing to come they were quite happy to give up.

Bobbie had always made the cakes for her tennis parties and thought she was quite accomplished at that. But her skill had depended on the cook making sure the oven was ready before she started. When her cook at Cucumgilliga went on holiday, and she had to use her basic skill more seriously, Bobbie realised what a big advantage this had been.

She had a wood stove similar to the one at Springfield, and these stoves needed much fine judgment to produce good results. The difficulty was in judging the temperature. Really good cooks could do this by instinct. They knew their oven and they were familiar with the wood they used. But for those less skilled it was a constant problem. The fire would either be too small, and the stove not hot enough, or it would be too large and the stove would take a long time to cool down to the required temperature. If you needed to use the oven and simmer something on the top at the same time you had to direct the heat as you needed it, and this was a tricky matter.

'The wood made such a difference too. At Cucumgilliga they used the local boxwood which burnt much better than the wood we had at Springfield. Once, when I was trying to get used to it, I put far too much wood on and the stove got so hot that I couldn't go near it! And once when I had a friend over from Goulburn we could not sit in the kitchen at all. It was very hot outside, middle of summer, and with the stove going as well the kitchen was simply unbearable. So we went and sat on the lino in the hall. I don't think I could ever have been a pioneer like my family!'

Cooking was, of course, a laborious process even for a professional cook, as there were few appliances to do the hard work. Mixing, blending, beating, juicing down, all were done by hand with a few basic tools. And variety came only from the changing season. When the carrots in the garden were ready, people ate carrots until they were finished and something else took their place. Vegetables came fresh

from the garden and so they had to be washed, peeled or shelled before they could be cooked.

Some foods could be preserved by pickling or bottling, but keeping those that couldn't was always a problem. When a sheep was killed for mutton all the meat had to be half cooked immediately so that it would keep. Even then it had only a limited life, especially in the summer. Some things that are easy now, such as getting a jelly to set in the summer, required much ingenuity. One cook used to put hers in the empty fireplace to get the down draught from the chimney, but even that was not always successful.

The kerosene refrigerator was indispensable and a vast improvement on the old Coolgardie safe which it replaced. It was about the size of a modern refrigerator, although its thick walls meant that its capacity was much less. Underneath it was a tank of kerosene and a wick similar to that on an oil lamp which was kept burning all the time. These refrigerators were remarkably efficient. There was, of

Bobbie Maple-Brown, right, at the Bong Bong picnic races about 1926.

course, no thermostat and if the door was not opened very often they simply became colder and colder.

Socially, the Cowra district proved disappointing to Bobbie. 'I was used to Goulburn, where everybody knew me. But here nobody knew us and it was a little lonely. One woman came to visit me and said in a very patronising voice that she thought we had quite a nice place. It seemed to surprise her. And then she said I should be glad to be living there because this was the best part of Australia. I thought to myself, "How ridiculous. Goulburn is much better".'

The high point of the year, apart from the Terranna Ball, was the trip to Sydney for the Countess of Dudley Cup, which was one of the main events in polo. Not only was the polo good, but so were the parties. One of these was always at Government House and on the first occasion this was the subject of some confusion. 'We were with a man who played in Irwin's team, and his wife. They were much older and remembered Government House before the war. She insisted that the men should wear white gloves and made them put them on in the taxi on the way there. But when we arrived she soon realised that none of the men were wearing gloves and she hissed to them to take them off. They said that they had only just put them on, but it didn't make any difference!'

Some years earlier Bobbie had been left a considerable sum of money by an uncle and she was to come into this money when she was twenty-five, or when she married if that happened earlier. Even at the modest rates of interest of those days, this money was enough to produce an income about six times greater than the average man's wage.

'It was marvellous, really, because it meant I always had money of my own. That must make marriage a lot easier, mustn't it? If I wanted to give Irwin a present I could do it with my money, rather than buying it with his and giving it back to him.'

She also bought a car for herself. 'It was the silliest little car, but I thought it was lovely. It was a Fiat, and I was terribly thrilled to have a car of my own. It was an open car, of course. We thought then that only people like Aunt Flory bought closed cars.'

The local roads were quite dreadful. The road to Boorowa, for example, was little more than a track that meandered through paddocks and across creeks and up hills. Some of these were so steep that when they were wet the car needed chains on the wheels in order to climb them. There were also thirty gates between Boorowa and Cowra and Bobbie once suggested to Irwin that the reason he had married her was to have somebody to open them for him.

During the winter it was difficult to drive at all. 'I said I was going out one winter's day and Irwin said I should not go. I thought, "Well, I'm not going to be told what I can do. Of course I can go out". So I did, and I skidded about all over the place. I've no idea how I ever got home, but I certainly saw what he meant.'

Irwin was a very good driver, and a fast one by those standards. 'I remember when we first did sixty miles an hour. We could hardly believe that. And then he drove from Gunning to Goulburn in an hour. That was forty-eight miles and people were almost speechless, you know.'

He also tried to improve Bobbie's driving technique, which sometimes made him despair. 'In those days you had to advance and retard the ignition depending on the nature of the road, and I must say it did improve the performance of the car. But my father never really understood it and when he taught me to drive he told me not to change it. So if I was driving, Irwin would often get annoyed and tell me to advance the ignition because the engine was labouring. "No," I would say, "Dad says not to move that." Isn't it silly when you think somebody is always right?'

In the end she did learn how to do it. Irwin also taught her to remember the road after he realised that she always hit the same pothole every time she drove to Cowra.

In 1924 Bobbie Maple-Brown was pregnant and needed more care than could be obtained locally. So Irwin sent her to relatives in Sydney and on 4 April 1925, at a nursing home in Killara, she was delivered of a son. They called him James.

When they returned to Cucumgilliga Irwin told Bobbie that he thought they might move. He and his thirty rabbiters had now practically eliminated the rabbits on the place, and that meant that Cucumgilliga could be sold at a good price. It might be time to take on another place that could be improved, and he had heard of one called Fonthill. It was in the small village of Lake Bathurst, which Bobbie knew well. It was only about eight miles from Springfield along the road to Braidwood, not far from Tarago.

Fonthill would be expensive to buy, and Irwin spent many hours in thoughtful calculation. Finally he said that if they got a good price for Cucumgilliga and its stock, and if they could organise a loan from the bank, they might just be able to manage. Bobbie was concerned about the size of the loan they would need, for her father had never had a loan on Springfield and she had long believed that you should only have what you could pay for. But if it could be made to work there was no doubt where she would rather be.

'Irwin told me that there was a railway line which ran through the front garden, and he thought I might be worried about that. I told him that did not matter at all. People could throw orange peel at me from the trains all day, so long as I was back in Goulburn!'

11
Fonthill

Bobbie was twenty-five when the family moved to Fonthill. They still owned Cucumgilliga at the time of the move and Irwin continued to run it from Fonthill. They had a manager at Cucumgilliga and the family made the journey from Fonthill nearly every weekend.

Although Fonthill was only eight miles from Springfield the country was noticeably different. Fonthill was on the edge of the plain that surrounded Springfield and the country was much more undulating. The range of hills that defined the boundary of the plain were much closer and had a greater effect on the local weather.

It was no more than a comfortable ride between the two, and Bobbie often went to Springfield, where her parents still lived in the Cottage and Aunt Flory continued to live alone in the big house. Although Springfield and Fonthill both fronted on to the same road it was easier, and much more pleasant, to ride across the country. 'You just rode through the paddocks. After you left Fonthill you rode through Inveralochy, which was owned by one of my cousins, and then you were almost at Springfield.'

But when she became pregnant again the riding had to come to an end and she went to Sydney for the birth of her second child. 'I had a daughter, and she was born on 15 May 1928 and we called her Diana. She was born in Macquarie street in a block of apartments called the Astor, which we thought was rather funny. I had to go and do it at the Astor!'

It was, though, a worrying time. Indeed, it was probably the only time in her life that Bobbie was ever anxious about money.

The problem was that as the recession started to make itself felt, so the values of properties started to drop. They had found it difficult to sell Cucumgilliga and in the end neither the property nor the stock brought the price they had expected. The result was that they had to take out a larger loan from the bank.

'I remember lying awake at night at Fonthill because we had borrowed such a lot of money to pay for it. It was nothing to do with me. It was Irwin's place, and he put into it the money he got from Cucumgilliga, which was also his. But I thought it would be such a disgrace if we failed. I suppose I knew that dad would never let that happen, and I had enough money for us all to live on anyway. Somebody once said to me that you wouldn't worry on it. But I did worry terribly about it.'

There was worse to come. As recession turned into depression the banks raised the interest rates, and those with large loans suddenly found themselves paying considerably more interest than they had ever anticipated.

Irwin went to Sydney to talk to his banker. The banker explained the reality of the situation, but not very sympathetically. 'You borrowed the money,' he said to Irwin, 'and now you will have to carry the baby.' But Irwin did not think it was as simple as that. 'You are only too willing to lend money when times are good. I think you should carry your share when times are bad.'

As a result of this meeting the bank agreed not to increase the interest on the loan, and their future at Fonthill was much more secure. But although Bobbie was very relieved, she was also uneasy about the special treatment they had received. 'If you were a little farmer out of Bourke and you didn't know anybody, you would have been worried to death when they put the interest up. There was a ruling brought in by the government that people could not be sold up because they couldn't pay the interest, but a lot of people had to leave just the same. They simply could not struggle on any further.'

Bobbie and Irwin were lucky to have a run of good seasons at Fonthill which allowed them to consolidate and before long they were

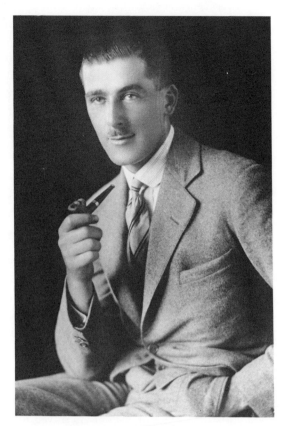

hardly dependent on the bank at all. 'My father had said when we took the place that he didn't think we would ever get it to pay. It was one of the few times he was wrong. When I said to him later that we had made £7000 from it in one year he could hardly believe it.'

The house at Fonthill was much more comfortable than that at Cucumgilliga, even though it lacked the splendour of the big house at Springfield. It was a large, rambling building, not unlike the distinctive houses in the Sydney suburb of Strathfield. It had lots of bay windows and verandahs and was covered in Victorian ornateness. Inside there was a long hall down the middle which led to a billiard room at the back, and beyond that was a complete wing containing more rooms than they were ever likely to use.

The house was surrounded by a large formal garden that was sheltered by the hills, while behind the house the hills formed gullies in the closer paddocks. One was covered in wild cherry trees, and Bobbie called it the Swiss Gully.

Houses like this were virtually impossible to run without staff. Indeed, nobody ever supposed they would have to be. Apart from the constant work in the kitchen, simply keeping the house clean kept several maids busy most of the time.

All the rooms, including the bedrooms, were swept with a carpet sweeper every day, and all the rooms were 'turned out' once a week. This was a big job, especially if the room was full of Victorian clutter, like the library at Springfield which Aunt Flory used as a sitting room.

There, the maid had to climb a step ladder in order to clear the high mantlepiece of all its photograph frames, vases, ornaments, boxes, bowls and glassware. All these were placed on the sofa and covered with a dust sheet. The maid then sprinkled damp rose petals on the floor if she had them, or small pieces of damp newspaper if she had not. These were then swept up with a straw broom and collected in a dust pan. The dust sheet was then removed from the sofa and all the ornaments were carefully dusted before being carried back up the step ladder and replaced in their correct position on the mantelpiece. It was a lengthy business and there were no short cuts.

At Fonthill Bobbie employed local girls as maids, some of whom were only fourteen years old. 'I used to try and train them and some of them turned out to be very good. One I remember became a very good cook and some of the others stayed for a long time.'

It could be confusing, though. One ram buyer who stayed for lunch turned out to be the uncle of the girl who was serving them. They shook hands and talked away until Bobbie thought she should ask the girl to sit down and have lunch with them.

There were also internal rules that had to be obeyed, for the hierarchy of domestic staff was almost as rigid as society itself. Duties were clearly defined and status was thus established. A cook, for example, would not expect to do housework except in very special circumstances, and only then as a favour. Even the maids had their own rules. The maid who looked after the ground floor at Fonthill would not clean the bottom step of the staircase because she insisted it was the job of the upstairs maid. The upstairs maid denied this, and said it belonged to the downstairs maid. The step was cleaned secretly by Bobbie for many years in order to keep the peace.

Bobbie always tried to look after her staff, and rarely had difficulty in keeping them. The house was usually quiet during the afternoon and Bobbie allowed the staff to play tennis on the court nearby. It was unusual, and quite appalled the trained nurse who had been brought in to look after Jimmy when he was sick. She said to Bobbie that the girls came rushing back into the house after playing tennis with barely enough time to cook dinner. But that didn't worry Bobbie. As long as they produced the dinner somehow she didn't care how long they were out.

'But a lot of people were terrible to their staff, I think. Maids had a weekend off once in six weeks and hardly any holidays, but people would still expect them to work day and night. I never saw any reason to keep them in the house during the afternoon. They were better to be out enjoying themselves. But some people would try to find more work for them, like polishing all the silver or something. I thought that was ridiculous. It really was a very hard life for them as it was. I think that is why I was something of a socialist when I was young.'

Just as some people could be depressingly hard on their staff, so elderly and professional staff could be dreadful bullies with young employers — like the cook who came from Sydney.

Irwin and Bobbie had decided to hold a house party for the Terranna weekend. It was the first they had ever held at Fonthill because previously they had spent that weekend at Springfield or Gundary Plains. As the house would be full of guests, therefore, Irwin suggested that Bobbie should bring a cook down from Sydney.

The cook seemed competent enough when she arrived, but the following morning Irwin asked Bobbie why the saucepans were scattered around the garden. She had no idea, but she soon found out. It appeared that one of the guests had made a cup of coffee the night before and had left the dirty saucepan in the kitchen. The cook was now hurling the rest through the kitchen window.

'When I spoke to her she told me to get out of her kitchen. So I told her that I thought it would be better if she left. "No," she said. She had come for a week, and she was going to stay for a week. Then she started swearing at me.'

Bobbie beat a retreat and Irwin took over. He did no better. When he came back from the kitchen, which still resounded to the crashing of saucepans, he said that she still would not go and he thought he had better call the policeman from Tarago.

By the time the policeman arrived the cook had gone to her bedroom. He explained that there was not much he could do, and perhaps Bobbie could try talking to her again. But the cook shouted through the closed door that she had no intention of leaving and when Bobbie said that a policeman had arrived she said, 'That doesn't worry me. I didn't walk out with a policeman for nothing.'

But when the policeman told the cook that she really would have to leave she finally burst into tears. She would go, she said, but not until she had had her bath. And she would 'have it proper too'.

When she was ready, Irwin and the jackeroo drove her into Goulburn to catch the train back to Sydney, thinking that would be safer than putting her on the train at Lake Bathurst. Irwin drove at great speed, as he usually did, and was embarrassed when she thanked him for hurrying. There had been no need, for her train did not leave for another two hours.

With the house still full of guests, Bobbie asked the agency in Sydney if they could supply another cook. They could, but she would want £4 a week. 'We thought that was a terrific amount, but Irwin said, "Get her. You have all these people staying and you can't possibly cook for them all".'

The new cook turned out to be worth every penny. 'She came off the Sydney train at five o'clock and she served a four course dinner at half past seven. And she was the nicest woman. We always had her back whenever we had a big party.'

In spite of their financial worries in the early years, Bobbie was very happy at Fonthill. 'I think there is always something special about the place where your children are young.'

Indeed, Jim and Diana were growing up in circumstances that were not all that much different to those that Bobbie had enjoyed at Springfield, except that their generation was in some ways more advanced. They certainly knew things at an earlier age than Bobbie had, and shocked people because of it. Diana once reprimanded a friend for handling a cat roughly. 'Can't you see that it is going to have kittens?' she said, and the cook nearly fainted.

They could even surprise Bobbie. One day they were burning logs in one of the paddocks and Bobbie said to Diana that they would leave

The house at Fonthill.

one large log because it would provide good shelter for a ewe when she was lambing. But when they returned they found that Jim had already set it alight. Diana accused him of being heartless and when Jim said that he really didn't think it mattered very much she said, 'It's all right for you. You would be the old ram and have all the fun!'

During the 1930s Irwin started to apply the new techniques of pasture improvement at Fonthill. In the past, grazing land had received little or no attention and had largely looked after itself. There had been no other way.

Now there was. If the land was cleared of all but essential shade trees, and if the soil was dressed with the new superphosphate and resown with special varieties of clover and grass, then the pasture could be made much more productive. This in turn meant that far more sheep could be supported by the pasture than had been possible before.

These new methods were not universally popular at that time. They were expensive, for one thing, and early attempts were not always successful. Exotic grasses might be abundant in good seasons but some had no resistance to drought and were the first to die when the season changed. The pasture would then seem far from 'improved' and might become almost unusable until the hardier native grasses re-established themselves.

Lucian Faithfull was one of the sceptics. 'Well,' he said, 'I like to see a young fellow with plenty of go, but of course you'll lose all your money on it.' And a cousin became quite angry on the subject and said they would ruin the place. He too thought they would lose everything. In which case, said Bobbie, one of them was sure to be happy. 'We'll be happy if it is a success, and you'll be happy if we go broke. He said I was hopeless to talk to, but there was nothing else to say, was there?'

As people learnt more of the techniques, pasture improvement became more certain and the results more predictable. It became a success and the dire forecasts were proved wrong, although it was many years before it was used on a wide scale.

While the thirties brought hardship and even misery for some, for Bobbie it was a very satisfying time.

'Although the Depression was still on, we really did think that things were beginning to change for the better. Working class people were getting a much better run than they had, and you felt better about that. I remember we once had an Englishman staying with us at Fonthill and he asked who it was driving a car round the place. I said it was the gardener and he was absolutely stunned that the gardener had a car. But by that time most of our people had been able to buy themselves a car.

'And we thought everything we were doing on the place, like clearing the trees and improving the pasture, was a great benefit. Not only to us, but for the whole of the country.'

12

The Second World War

IF THE START of the First World War had taken Bobbie, and even her father, by surprise, the coming of the Second World War was much more visible.

Throughout most of the thirties the newspapers reported a succession of aggressive acts by Germany and her allies. Italy invaded Ethiopia in 1935-36 and Germany annexed Austria and Sudetenland in 1938. Closer to home, Japan conquered Manchuria in 1931 and invaded China in 1937.

Even so, the threat to Australia seemed remote. If there was to be another war, then Australian troops would fight alongside the British as they had before. Few even thought to doubt that, and even fewer thought that the war would come any closer than the last one. Indeed, when Neville Chamberlain returned from Munich in 1938 to tell cheering crowds in England that he had brought 'peace with honour' it seemed to many people that there might not even be a war at all.

But there were some who were less optimistic. There were even some in Australia who thought that not only would there be a war, but the involvement of Japan would put Australia at risk in a way that had not happened before.

Irwin Maple-Brown was one of these people. Not only would there be another war, he said, but there was a real possibility that Japan would invade Australia.

By 1938 he thought it was time to be doing something about it. Trained men would be needed in large numbers, and he knew that they could not be trained over night. When the need became obvious, it might already be too late.

Irwin was faced with a dilemma. Men who worked the land would be as valuable doing that as they would be in the forces. The country would still need agricultural products and those skilled in supplying them could do a job that others could not do. Perhaps he would be more valuable producing wool for uniforms than he would be carrying a rifle.

'Although Irwin had no doubt what was going to happen, not many people seemed to think much about it at that time. I think it was the events after Munich that brought it home to most people.'

It was then that Bobbie and Irwin spent a whole afternoon discussing what he should do. He said that he thought they would take him in the Light Horse, but he still was not sure whether he should go or not. 'He said that if the Japanese did come, England would not be able to offer much help and we would have to look after ourselves. Personally, I couldn't see what the Light Horse might hope to do either. But I did say that if he thought there was going to be a war maybe it was better to go early.'

By the end of the afternoon he had made his decision. He would join the army reserve. He went outside as the men at Fonthill were finishing work for the day and told them what he was going to do. Perhaps some of them would like to join too. 'Oh, well, if you are going, Mr Irwin, we'll go with you,' they said. They had, as Bobbie said, not even talked to their wives.

They were also ahead of their time. Although they joined the Seventh Light Horse shortly afterwards they were to be trained on a part-time basis because the army at that time was not capable of absorbing a large number of recruits. That was to come later. Instead, the new men would be trained in camps when they were needed and the rest of the time they would continue to work at Fonthill.

The first camp was to last ten days and although war had still not been declared it gave Bobbie an indication of what was to come.

'It was the longest ten days of my life, although it doesn't sound very dramatic now. All the men disappeared except for a couple who were too old, and I was left to look after the place. There wasn't much warning either. One week there was a full staff and the next week I was running the place with two men.'

One of her first jobs was to ride around the paddocks treating fly-blown sheep. Flies were a perpetual hazard and in those days there were no effective measures to prevent them attacking sheep. Blowflies, particularly numerous in wet weather, laid their eggs in the skin of the sheep and these eggs hatched into a loathsome mass of maggots that lived as parasites on the sheep. The treatment was to cut the fly-blown wool from the sheep and to treat the skin with disinfectant. It was an unpleasant job and even experienced station hands showed little enthusiasm for it.

'I took Diana with me. She was ten at the time and her job was to catch the sheep and hold them while I clipped the wool off with a pair of hand shears. She was very critical too. She kept telling me that I wasn't doing it correctly and that I wasn't holding the shears the way Irwin had shown me. I said it didn't matter so long as I could get the wool off!'

If the war had started with part-time soldiers, and not many of those, that changed when Paris fell in 1940. By then even the most optimistic had to accept that this war was going to be every bit as nasty as the last and those of Irwin's friends who had been surprised when he joined the army in 1938 now rushed to do the same.

Irwin's views had changed too and he now wanted to resign his commission in the Light Horse so that he could join a regiment that might be more active. This turned out to be a difficult thing to do, but in 1940 he was able to transfer to the Eleventh Armoured Cars. A part-timer no more, he left Fonthill to join them at their base at Puckapunyal in Victoria.

'My whole life changed so much in a short time that I could hardly believe it. Before Irwin joined the Light Horse I was having a lovely time with the children. We used to take a picnic and go riding up in the hills. I loved doing that, and they used to enjoy it too. But then they got older and one day they asked me rather hesitantly if I would mind if they went on their own. I was really very disappointed, but they were old enough to do that and you have to take a different attitude when children start to grow up.'

Indeed, the house at Fonthill was very full at that time. There was Jim and Diana and their governess, and then there was Irwin's father. He had suffered a stroke and his doctor thought he might do better if he was at Fonthill. There was also his nurse, and Irwin's younger brother who was working there.

'I remember sneaking out of the house one afternoon hoping that nobody would see me. I just wanted to ride over the hills by myself. I succeeded in getting away and felt much better when I came back.'

But a year later it was quite different. Irwin was at Puckapunyal, his brother had died, his father was in hospital in Sydney, and the two children were at boarding school. 'Then I never saw anybody. Talk about a change!'

She was left with three men to run Fonthill. 'One, fortunately, was the overseer, who had sinus trouble. The second was too old to go, and the third went peculiar if he had a drink so his wife thought he should stay on the place instead, which he could do because of his job.'

She also had the help of Harry Dunn, a highly respected sheep man who had been a protégé of Lucian Faithfull. On Lucian's suggestion, Irwin had taken Harry Dunn into partnership with the sheep to help him establish the Fonthill stud on pure Springfield blood.

Harry Dunn, who was too old for military service, and the overseer were probably the saving of the place. Dunn continued to class the rams and supervise the breeding programme while the overseer, who was very experienced with stock, organised the small staff so that Fonthill could continue to function. But Bobbie still had to be in the paddocks for much of the time, especially when the ewes were lambing.

'I spent a lot of time doing that on my own and I think I became quite good at it. Once I had this ewe and I couldn't lamb her and I knew I needed some help. So before I left her I tied some handkerchieves I had with me around her head. When I found the overseer he said he would go himself and asked me where she was. He found her all right and he saved the lamb, but he was intrigued by all the handkerchieves. He thought I had put them there so he could recognise her, but it wasn't for that at all. It was because of the crows. If the ewe was down on the ground the crows would come and attack their eyes. I thought the handkerchieves would protect her, and they did.'

In 1941 Jim came home from school to add his strength for a while, and to be on hand to help move dairy cattle from the south coast of New South Wales should there be a Japanese invasion.

For Bobbie, this was the worst part of the war. Like most wives of property owners, she had seen her life change from the hustle and bustle of the pre-war years to one that was now almost monastic but which carried much more responsibility. She tried to make the best of things and remain cheerful, but she always had a clear understanding of what might happen.

At that time the outcome of the war was far from certain in Europe, and even less certain as far as Australia was concerned. The bombing of Pearl Harbour and Darwin, and the fall of Singapore in 1942, meant that a Japanese invasion of Australia was very likely.

One day when she was cooking breakfast a man came in and said that the Japanese were in Sydney Harbour. Irwin had already told her what to do if that happened. She was to take all the supplies she could, and the children if they were at home, and take refuge in the surrounding hills. Bobbie had not thought it a very good idea — 'I thought you might as well be the first to be shot as the last' — and when she discovered that the Japanese had already been destroyed in their midget submarines there was no need to take any action of that kind. But it was a frightening moment, shared by countless women whose husbands were away.

There is no doubt that many wives suffered much more in the war than Bobbie did. They lost husbands and sons, or endured long years when they were overseas. Bobbie faced none of that and knows she was lucky. She was never called upon to be heroic. But, like almost everybody else, she did have to change her whole way of life, and there was nothing to be gained by complaining about it. Later, Jim decided to join up too. 'He could have stayed to run the place, and we really did need him. But one day in 1943 he said to me, "Look, I can't stay here living a normal life when all those fellows are in New Guinea and other places. I think they might take me in the Air Force".' They did.

By this time, most of Bobbie's domestic staff had left to work in factories and she was now left with a single maid. 'It is the nearest I have ever been to running a big house by myself. Of course, with

Aunt Flory, as a young woman and in old age.

everybody away there was not so much to do, but nobody had thought of anything that was labour saving when they built those places.'

There was also rationing. And even the things that were not rationed were hardly ever available. The house at Fonthill, like the big house at Springfield, was lit by gas from a carbide plant in the garden. The gas had, indeed, once nearly destroyed the house. One evening, when she was alone with the children, Bobbie had tried to light the mantle in one of the bedrooms. But instead of lighting, the mantle had exploded and started a small fire. She managed to put the fire out with a pillow, but the mantle had come off the wall and there was no way of turning the gas off. She eventually stopped it by ramming a cork down the pipe.

Later, though, she was unable to get the carbide which the plant needed and the gas supply came to an end. 'I had to go back to using kerosene lamps and we had them for quite a few years then. I remember that when Irwin came home on leave once he was able to get some carbide from somewhere and he started up the gas plant again. I thought that was marvellous. I had a light again and I had a husband for a few days. I thought the war was nearly over!'

Rationing was less of a problem because they had a big advantage of being able to produce most of their own food. It was the things they could not produce that caused the problems. There were 'ways' of obtaining such things, but she would have nothing to do with them.

Jim, who was with the air force at Wagga, had managed to make his car run on a mixture of shellite and kerosene and stocked up with them whenever he was able to come home. 'I was in the general store in Goulburn one day and I asked for a tin of kerosene for Jimmy, who was hoping to get back to Fonthill for a few days. The man, who I knew well, said that there was a new regulation and that I would have to sign a form to say that it would be used in lamps. Well, we did use it in lamps, but that was not what this was for and so I said I couldn't sign the form. I did some more shopping while he loaded the car and when I got back there was the tin of kerosene in the boot. I thought I should take it back, but I didn't. So in the end I was no better than anybody else.'

The continuing anxiety, of course, was that the men would suddenly be posted overseas. That was regarded as inevitable, so that whatever time they had left in Australia became very precious.

Fortunately the one thing Fonthill had a reasonable supply of was petrol. One of the first things Bobbie had to do when the war started was to fill in a form stating the minimum amount of petrol the place needed to continue its operations. Bobbie worked it out as best she could and was about to complete the form when the bookkeeper told her to double the amount. Because of the work in improving the pastures they had been using a great deal of petrol before the war and that figure would justify a high amount now. In any case, he pointed out, the authorities would simply halve whatever figure she supplied. It did, indeed, happen to a woman who had a property a few kilometres from Goulburn. She had been patriotic and filled in a true figure, but the authorities cut it so much that she didn't have enough petrol to keep the place going and she had to move into Goulburn.

Although Bobbie's allocation was also cut, she was able to use horses for transport and cartage and managed to have enough petrol to meet Irwin whenever the chance arose. At first that was quite frequent. When he was at Puckapunyal he discovered that he would be able to get to Melbourne most weekends and he asked her to meet him there. Not only that, but she could drive down in the ute and leave that with him while she returned by train. He would then be able to drive to Fonthill whenever he had the chance.

The only problem, she discovered, was that you needed a permit from the police before you could drive across the border at Albury. So she explained to the sergeant in Goulburn that she wanted a permit so she could take a car to her husband at Puckapunyal. He was very sorry, but that was not sufficient reason for him to issue her a permit. But he happened to know that the border, which was just past the bridge over the Murray, was never manned at night.

She set off with Jess Harris, one of the daughters of the manager of Springfield, and they reached Albury late in the afternoon. They then waited until it was dark and furtively drove over the bridge and past the deserted guard post with all the stealth of gun runners.

In practice, though, Irwin found it impractical to return to Fonthill, so whenever she could Bobbie travelled to join him either at his camp or in the nearest town so that they could spend some time together. 'So I became a camp follower, and it completed my education, I think.'

As Irwin moved from one camp to the next, Bobbie travelled by train across most of eastern Australia to spend her time with him. One day he phoned from Tamworth to say he would be having a day off. So Bobbie caught the night train from Sydney, which was full of school children being evacuated for fear of an invasion, and after a brief day with Irwin she started the long journey back to Fonthill.

'We still expected him to be sent overseas at any time, so you took every opportunity that came. As it happens, he never did go overseas. They said he was too old for that and offered him a job looking after an airfield, which quite disgusted him but made me very happy.'

She met a great many wives who also travelled long distances to spend time with their husbands, and learnt a great deal from them. 'They came from all kinds of background and it simply didn't matter. I had never been a believer in that awful class thing that the older people used to think was so important, but even if I had I am sure I would have changed then. We were all in the same boat, you know. We were never sure that we would see our husbands again.'

She was also amused by the different class structure of the army. 'There was a colonel's wife who thought she was very grand, and that was rather sad, really. She used to talk to people in a very patronising way just because of her husband's rank. Some of the wives were really very wealthy people and their husbands owned big properties which they had left to join up, but it didn't make any difference to her. Being a colonel's wife was much more important, she thought. She hardly ever gave me a second glance!'

But even she might have done so later. In 1942, after a long and trying illness, Lucian Faithfull passed away. And when his will was read it surprised nobody to learn that Bobbie Maple-Brown was the new owner of Springfield.

13
The Mistress of Springfield

Having inherited Springfield after her father's death in 1942 Bobbie thought they should continue to live at Fonthill, at least for the time being. Fonthill was, after all, Irwin's place and she thought that was where the family belonged. Not only that, but the shortage of staff at Fonthill made it almost impossible to run without her direct involvement.

Springfield, on the other hand, was running well in spite of the war. Mr Harris was still the manager and there were enough old members of the staff to keep the place functioning. A few younger men had also elected to stay on the place as an alternative to joining the forces. Some, indeed, were given no choice. They were sent home as soon as they tried to enlist.

Not that Bobbie was ever away from Springfield for long. Aunt Flory was now nearly ninety and needed constant care from Bobbie. Still alone in the big house, she had a personal staff which consisted of a cook, a parlour maid and a house maid. Outside, four or five men looked after the garden, and the vegetable garden that was only slightly smaller. Bobbie went to see her every few days. She usually saved petrol by riding across the paddocks as she had years ago.

Bobbie's mother continued to live in the Cottage, although it was already clear that she did not wish to stay there much longer. She had moved there in 1895 when she married Lucian and the place had too many memories to be comfortable now. She had four maids and a gardener, but the rambling house that Lucian had built for her was now much bigger than she needed.

After Lucian Faithfull's death, Irwin left the army and returned to run Fonthill. Irwin had a skin allergy from exposure to sheep dip and this had become worse in the army so that he was now no longer fit for active service. He also thought that he would be of more service using his specialised skills as a grazier than by looking after an airfield, a job which could, after all, be done by many people in the army at that time. In due course the authorities agreed that Irwin would be able to do a more productive job at home and agreed to his discharge.

It was 1944, then, before they at last decided to move on to Springfield. By then it seemed that the war might not last much longer and that there might, after all, be a future to plan for. It was also clear that Springfield now needed more attention than Fonthill. The fact was that as Lucian had grown older, so Springfield had lost some of its excellence. He had always believed that his sheep were second to none, but sadly this was no longer true.

By this time Irwin had improved the pastures at Fonthill to such an extent that they were capable of carrying twice as many sheep as they had supported when he had taken his family there in 1925. Springfield, on the other hand, had not been improved at all and Irwin, looking for a new challenge, thought it was time to start.

So in 1944 Bobbie moved back into the Cottage where she had been born and raised. Mrs Irwin, Miss Florence that was who had left after her marriage in 1923, returned home twenty-one years later as the mistress of Springfield.

Nothing much had changed, for the timelessness of Springfield had protected it from the Second World War as it had during the First. Not even modernity had encroached very far. Part of the big house was still lit by gas made in the carbide plant near the summer house, while the rest continued to rely on kerosene lamps. And over in the Cottage the generator continued to provide electricity for lighting, but nothing else. It was welcome, though, because it was the first domestic electricity Bobbie had had since she had left home.

Hot water in both houses, indeed all the houses, was still produced by wood-fired boilers, and fires were still used for heating as well. During the winter there were at least two fires burning all day to heat Aunt Flory's rooms, and there was always one in the Cottage. Houses used by the staff also needed wood fires and all needed functional fires for cooking and heating water. Sometimes even the supply of water depended on a fire. Domestic water was normally pumped out of the river by a windmill, but if there was no wind a man had to light a steam engine and then spend the rest of the day feeding it with wood. Springfield used so much firewood that it could no longer meet its own needs and much of it was now bought in.

In spite of the lack of change, though, Springfield was a magical place, and as the war drew to an end it still had a role to play. In June 1945 Bobbie and Irwin threw Springfield open to a party of sailors from the Royal Navy whose ships were then in Sydney Harbour. It was typical of many visits of this kind that were arranged by landowners to show their appreciation for those who were fighting the war in far less pleasant surroundings.

The sailors spent the day enjoying life on a sheep station, certainly the first most of them had ever seen. They rode horses, and fell off them to the cheers of their mates who called 'land oh!' when the inevitable occurred. They were surprised, they said, that Irwin Maple-Brown, who was already a distinguished polo player, and his son Jim did not seem to have any difficulty staying on.

They explored the woolshed and were surprised to learn that after the wool had been cut off the sheep, they were sent back into the paddocks to grow it again so that it could be cut off once more the following year. 'Heck,' said one of them, 'I'd turn that in.'

But by the end of the day they knew something of the charm of Springfield, and many remembered it for a long time. As one said when he was leaving, 'Those game, old-boy pioneers must have loved this country just as much as England, or perhaps it's just that they couldn't have loved one without the other. I think I know how they felt, for I feel the same way now.'

Springfield at that time consisted of fourteen thousand acres (5,740 hectares) and ran about eleven thousand sheep. There was a staff of twenty, but with wives and families nearly ninety people lived on Springfield. One of the staff was the fourth generation of his family to work there and he promised that he would be around for a long time yet. The village now consisted of about twenty houses, together with dozens of service buildings. It was, in fact, about the size of the village of Lake Bathurst which Bobbie and Irwin had recently left.

Springfield was also nearly capable of supporting itself. The large garden provided a constant supply of fruit and vegetables, while at the back of the big house the dairy produced milk and cream. This produce, together with a weekly supply of mutton, was provided to the staff as part of the award wage.

Nor had attitudes changed much either. 'It was still a very feudal turn out when we came back, although it did start to change a little after that.'

But the pressures for change were at first no match for the traditional ways. One man who went there to work was amused at the ritual that took place at the start of each working day. The men would assemble at the corner of the coach house and wait for Irwin to come through the gate from his office. As he did so he would say, 'Good morning, men', and the men would reply in unison, 'Good morning, Mr Irwin'.

'Well, I wasn't going to join in that. So the next day I didn't say anything, just looked at the ground or something. So after the men had said, "Good morning, Mr Irwin", he looked at me and said, "And good morning, Harry". It fixed me. "Good morning, Mr Irwin," I said, and I said it with the best of them every morning after that!'

The school too was as traditional as it had always been, and still as necessary. 'I think dad liked to take on men with families so that the school could keep going. But the original school had become too small, so he converted that into the schoolmaster's house and built another school further up the hill.'

At the end of each term the school put on a play in the woolshed and Bobbie and Irwin invariably sat in the front row. 'I don't know how it started. They just seemed to leave those seats for us every time, as if that was where we were supposed to sit.'

It was part of the ritual. When a new family attended for the first time and the wife sat in one of those seats she was promptly moved by the others. 'She must be a very ignorant women,' said one of the other wives, and insisted it was so even when Bobbie said there was no way she could have known. And when a new, younger schoolmaster

Part of the big house at Springfield after the renovation.

took over he asked Bobbie whether they usually sat in a special place. She explained the custom to him and he said, 'Oh, that's all right. I'm just not familiar with these old-fashioned ways'.

'You know, I think the older ones liked the old ways. It's different now, isn't it? I suppose it's better, really, better for everybody. But I don't think the old hands minded as much as people think they did now.'

Some of these changes were, indeed, brought about by Bobbie. It had, for example, been the custom for her mother to buy the school prizes and to present them after the play, and at first Bobbie did the same. 'But I really didn't like doing it because it seemed so paternalistic. So Jimmy and I thought it would be better if the Parents and Citizens did that. I made a donation and they bought the prizes, which I think was a much better idea.'

She also campaigned for longer holidays for the men. At that time they had two weeks' holiday every year. 'I thought that was very mean and I suggested to Irwin that we give them three weeks. He said he supposed we could and we decided that any man who had been with us for ten years, which was most of them, could have three weeks' holiday a year. We thought we were very forward-thinking, but not long after that there was a rule that everybody had to have a month. How quickly things altered!'

She had been very concerned about Irwin's attitude towards the men when they moved on to Springfield, for his approach was quite different to Lucian Faithfull's. 'I thought Irwin would sack the lot. Dad had never put a man off in his life, I think, and the place was always overstaffed. So I thought it wouldn't be long before Irwin started cutting them down to his level. Dad had also told me that Mr Harris could stay at Springfield as long as he wanted to. I was a bit worried about that too, because I knew Irwin would not need a manager in the way dad had. But Mr Harris was quite old when we came down. He had been there nearly fifty years and he said he was ready to retire.'

Her other anxiety was how Irwin would get on with Aunt Flory. Although she was not involved in running Springfield she still had her own staff to look after the big house and to run the gardens. Although this was a separate operation, there were areas where these functions overlapped.

One was the handling of the mail. The custom was for the mail to be laid out in the hall of the big house, where it was collected by some of the staff and outgoing mail left with the money for the postage. It was all very casual, and there was a risk that a child might seize the opportunity and make off with the money that had been left there. In any case it meant those collecting or leaving the mail had to go into the house to do so.

Irwin thought it should be changed, and suggested to Aunt Flory that they make some pigeon holes that could be fixed to an outside wall at the back of the house. No, she said. The mail had always been handled her way, and it would be handled that way until she died. Irwin said to Bobbie, 'Well, I suppose we had better keep on doing it like that', and the moment past.

To her surprise, Irwin didn't fire many staff either — only one, and that was Aunt Flory's chauffeur. During the war the chauffeur had little to do because of the scarcity of petrol and because Aunt Flory rarely went out now. His only job was to look after a small part of the lawn near the house, and to take Aunt Flory's nurse into Goulburn. The petrol, he said, would allow only one trip one month and two the next. Unfortunately he made the mistake of waving at the men one day as he drove past them, working in the full sun on countless hundreds of sheep.

Irwin suggested to Aunt Flory that as there was a war on she might feel the man should do a little more about the place. Not in the paddocks, but perhaps he could do more in the garden. She agreed, but when Irwin told the man of the change he said that he was on her staff and he would not take orders from him. That was his second mistake. There never was a third.

Although Irwin worked the men hard, he was seen to be fair and more than competent and they all got on well together.

It was, at that time, still difficult for a man to leave a property anyway. There was a convention among landowners that they would not employ a man who was still employed elsewhere. Indeed, Irwin had himself fallen foul of this convention when he was at Fonthill. He had visited a neighbouring property to see a man who said he had given notice. It turned out to be not true. 'The owner was very indignant and thought it was a terrible thing to do. There was a great fuss and my father said that it was quite right, you should never do that. Well, I thought that was very mean. How can a man get away if he hasn't got another job to go to?'

If a man wanted to leave Springfield, Irwin was ready to help him provided he knew him to be a good man. It might seem a small matter now, but at that time it was almost revolutionary.

There were other changes, too, after the war. One was the idea that large landholders should have some of their land resumed and this should be made available for returned servicemen. This had been done after the First World War and it had been a popular move even though the results were not always very successful.

When it was decided to do the same after the Second World War, Bobbie Maple-Brown, owner of Springfield, was all in favour and thought that if everybody surrendered some land voluntarily it would avoid much of the bitterness that it had caused before.

'As a matter of fact we practically offered them some land because we still had Fonthill and I thought we could do with less. I might say my father would have turned in his grave. He wasn't narrow minded about most things, but he was about the Labor Party. If it rained when he was shearing he used to think it was their fault. He told me that I should never let anybody cut the place up because they made the blocks too small to be successful.'

A man who sat next to Bobbie on the bus one day seemed to know all the answers. Bobbie often used the bus for her trips to Goulburn in order to conserve petrol. The bus came out on the Braidwood road and there was a stop near one of the Springfield gates. There was then a lengthy walk to the Cottage, but it was a pleasant one if the weather was comfortable.

On this occasion the man she was sitting next to thought, like many people on country buses, that conversation made the journey much shorter. As the bus drove past Terranna he asked Bobbie if she knew how it had got its name. No, she didn't. 'Well,' he said, 'the first owner used to shear his own sheep and if he cut one he used to call for his wife, who was called Anna, to bring him the bucket of tar. Terranna.' 'That is very interesting,' she said.

The road from there ran across the large flat plain which was part of Springfield. 'Of course,' the man said, 'this ought to be all cut up. It is disgraceful. It is all land-locked.' 'Oh,' said Bobbie, 'I think they could get better land than that for the returned men. There is no permanent water on that plain and hardly any trees.' 'I don't know anything about that,' he said, 'but everybody says it ought to be cut up.'

Bobbie got off the bus at the gate a little further on and when she turned round to close it she was surprised to see everybody in the bus staring at her. She discovered later that the driver had said to the man that he might be interested to know that he had just told the owner of Springfield that she should give up half her land.

Nor did his earlier story have any truth. 'When I got home I told mother what he had said, and she said, "How ridiculous. Her name was Alice!"'

Springfield lost several thousand acres to soldier settlement after the war, and Bobbie changed her mind. 'I think my father was right because I discovered that it really was all political. They could have got much better places out on the western plains, but here they made the blocks too small, just like he said. There is only one of the original men left there now.'

Meanwhile, Irwin set about improving Springfield in the way he had at Fonthill, and the first step was to clear it of surplus trees. Lucian Faithfull had never removed trees unless they had died of natural causes. Nor had they presented much of a problem. The plain had always been open country with hardly any trees, but elsewhere, and especially near the ranges to the west, there were a considerable number of them.

'Irwin left enough shade trees standing to protect the stock and then cleared most of the rest. I thought it was a shame in a way because they did make the place look so beautiful, and he did agree to leave a line of them that ran along one of the boundary fences. But you had to clear them so that you could plant the subterranean clover which made the pasture so much better.'

The need was greater now than it had been at Fonthill. Increasing costs after the war meant that properties had to be run more productively if they were to survive. The days when Springfield could carry any number of staff and still make money were coming to an end. They were now in a more competitive market and the cost of running the place was far higher than it had been in Lucian's time.

The way to increase the productivity of Springfield was to run more sheep on it. And the way to do that safely was to improve the quality of the pasture that supported them.

'We thought we were improving the place out of sight. Now, it seems to be rather doubtful. You had to do it then so that you could run enough stock to make the place pay, but I don't think they are using as much super now. It washes into the creeks, and because you have more stock you have more manure washing in as well. It seems to be a matter of degree, but at that time it was still fairly new and exciting.'

The drawing room at Springfield.

There was also a heavy programme of maintenance, which had inevitably been neglected during the war. Even now it was difficult to carry out because many materials were still scarce, but as they became available fences were mended, new yards built, sheds and houses repainted and machinery replaced.

'The houses were a big problem. Dad always said that if he hadn't had the place he would have been an architect, but he was the worst builder you ever saw. Even the cottages he built in 1910 didn't have any bathrooms. They were very nice, built of solid brick and with good living areas and kitchens, but he always seemed to forget about bathrooms. So we had to start improving them, and that was a big job.'

Irwin was also aware that he needed to introduce new blood into the flock and said he would be going to the Sydney Show to buy a new ram. Although that was the usual way of going about it, Bobbie didn't think it was such a good idea. 'Well, I knew from my father how people got their rams up for the show. I'm not saying there is anything wrong in it, but it is obviously done to make the ram look perfect and to hide any faults it might have. So I said to Irwin that he might do better by looking on somebody's place. Then he would see the rams in their natural state. But I don't think he ever got round to buying one in the end. I don't think he was quite brave enough because my father was so proud that he hadn't had any new blood for years.'

If Irwin did not buy rams, he did buy horses. He was a keen supporter of the local picnic races, even though Terranna was no more, and liked to have a number of runners at most of them. During a trip to Sydney not long after the war, Irwin and Jim went to the Newmarket sales and bought several promising mares in one day. They intended to go the following day and do the same again. Bobbie objected. They had already bought enough and she would go with them tomorrow to put a stop to it.

'So I went with the firm intention of stopping them buying any more horses, but then I saw a stallion called Tetreen and I asked Irwin if he liked him. Yes, he said, he thought he was a very good sort. So I said, "I'll go you halves if you buy him", and he couldn't believe his ears. But at least he did buy him.'

Tetreen was not expensive as a stallion, 'only a few hundred, not thousands like they pay now', nor did he live very long. But he was certainly very productive. One of their mares produced a foal by him that they called Alinga who soon won so many picnic races that it was no longer practical to enter him for them. Alinga later won the Sydney Gold Cup and when he then went to run in Brisbane, Bobbie and Irwin went to watch him.

'That is the only time I ever put some money on. I put £30 on him and when they were coming around the corner practically the whole of the grandstand was calling "Alinga". I shut my eyes and when I opened them he had come fourth. They said he got bumped, but they always tell you something, don't they?'

Alinga was being set for the Melbourne Cup when he fell in a race in Sydney and broke his leg. 'He eventually had to be destroyed. There didn't seem any point in trying to keep him alive in pain. I couldn't do that to an animal, even though they said he might live.

And do you know, people wrote to us saying they would keep him in their paddock. As if we wouldn't have done that! But it would have been cruel.'

They owned other horses too, but none were as successful as Alinga. One was called Nightgown because, Bobbie said, she was so easy to pull up.

In 1949 Aunt Flory died at the age of ninety-nine and another era at Springfield came to an end. She had lived in the big house since before Bobbie was born and had come to be 'the grand old lady of Springfield'. 'She really was a marvellous person. She had been ill for several years but she was as bright as a button right to the end.'

She was the last of Lucian's sisters, and with her death the big house now became part of Springfield again.

'My mother had left the Cottage by then and was living in Goulburn. So now we had to decide what to do. We had sold some of the land and the house at Fonthill and Jimmy was running what remained of that. He was still living at Springfield and used to go up there every day. But now we had to think of the big house as well as the Cottage. We obviously could not live in both. We thought it would be more appropriate to live in the big house, but we knew it would need an awful lot doing to it and we didn't know if we could take it on. On the other hand, my grandfather had built it as the Springfield homestead and we couldn't pretend it wasn't there. We would have to look after it even if we didn't live in it.'

By then graziers were getting the best prices for wool that they had ever seen. At one pound a pound, there was more money coming in than had ever seemed possible a few years earlier. Many spent lavishly and the legends of graziers bringing a couple of ewes from the paddock in the back of a Rolls Royce had their origin at this time.

For Bobbie and Irwin, it seemed a good time for a break. Apart from their honeymoon and the weekends together during the war they had not been away since their disastrous trip to New Zealand in 1921. Bobbie, the enthusiastic traveller, had been fairly stationary while she brought up her children and coped with the problem of running a property without a husband.

With the children now grown up, Bobbie and Irwin decided to go to England for a holiday, and to decide where they would live when they returned.

14

A Trip to England, and a Decision to Make

Eᴀʀʟʏ ɪɴ 1950 Bobbie, Irwin and Diana left Springfield for Sydney, where they were to join the ship for England. It was now possible to fly to England, although not many people did. The flight took several days because most aircraft landed at night so that the passengers could spend the night in comfort in a local hotel. Flying to England was much more expensive than going by ship, and only those who had to be there in a hurry thought the expense was worth the discomfort.

Ships were much more comfortable now. They were cool, clean and spacious and prided themselves in the service they offered. And a majestic liner was still given an enthusiastic send-off from Sydney, for 'going home' was still a big event. It was a golden era which came to an end when long distance air travel finally became faster, cheaper, and less excruciating.

London had changed too. Much of it, of course, had been reduced to rubble by German bombs and the scars were still visible. The docks, the East End and the area around St Pauls had all been devastated, while smaller scars could be found almost everywhere else. The Houses of Parliament and Victoria Station had both received direct hits and other, less famous, buildings had disappeared completely.

The war had been followed by a period of austerity. Many war-time restrictions still applied and after the jubilation of 1945 many people wondered if it had been worth all the effort and sacrifice. Petrol and food were still scarce and luxuries were almost unknown. Many children who had been born just before the war were ten or twelve years old before they saw their first fresh banana, and most had no idea how to remove the skin.

But by 1950 this was changing at last and after ten years of struggle there was now a feeling of optimism. Damaged buildings were being rebuilt and areas that had been nearly obliterated were being cleared away for massive new developments. On the south bank of the Thames near Waterloo Bridge the first non-essential development was already taking shape. It was the site of the Festival of Britain, to be held the following year, which would celebrate Britain's post-war achievements.

Although the war damage had been so massive that even a city as old and as big as London could not take it lightly, there were still parts of London that had hardly changed at all. Immaculate guardsmen still rode across the park to change the guard at Buckingham Palace as they had for generations. And from the park itself the soft, misty sunlight now gave peace to the city beyond. Among the trees or beside the lake it was still possible to find tranquillity, even in the middle of a city that had a population greater than the whole of Australia.

Bobbie was enchanted with it, just as she had been in 1914.

It was a busy time and not all of it would be spent in London. They intended to travel around the country and then to cross over to Scandinavia, which Bobbie had not visited before. But even she had not expected Irwin's announcement that he was going to buy a Bentley. 'I think you are mad. They will put up the prices wherever we go. What do you want a Bentley for?' 'You always wanted the trip,' he said, 'and I have always wanted a Bentley. We are going to have both.'

So they travelled around the country, mostly from one horse show to the next, in the comfort of a new Bentley. It was not very suitable for the job, though, as they had to load most of the luggage on the roof.

The museum which Bobbie made while renovating the house.

One day when they were in London Bobbie took a phone call from somebody who wanted to speak to Irwin. It was Lord Cowdrey and he wondered if Irwin would care to play polo. 'Irwin was out on business, but I said I really didn't think he could because he had not brought any clothes or equipment. "Well," Lord Cowdrey said, "Come out anyway and make yourselves known." '

So they did. And when Irwin saw the magnificent grounds of Cowdrey Park the temptation was too much. 'The polo in Australia after the war wasn't very good, so of course he couldn't resist playing again.'

But Bobbie had not travelled halfway around the world to watch Irwin play polo, which she had been doing for years at home anyway.

No, she said, she would take Diana to Norway, Sweden and Denmark as they had planned and Irwin could play polo and join them when he had finished.

He eventually caught up with them in Norway. 'I asked him if he had enjoyed the polo and he said, "Oh, yes. I won a cup".' She thought that very unlikely, but it was true. His team had beaten that of Lord Louis Mountbatten and the cup Irwin had won had been presented to him by Princess Elizabeth. 'But I don't think Lord Louis is supposed to be beaten.' 'Well, we beat him!'

It was almost the end of the trip. From Norway they flew back to London in what was their first international flight, and from there the family, a Bentley, and a polo cup started the voyage back to Australia.

They had intended to spend some time while they were away in deciding where they would live when they returned to Springfield, but there never seemed to be much time for that. It was not until they were back home that they thought about it in earnest.

Jim Maple-Brown had recently married Pamela Calder in Sydney and they were now living in the Harris's house at Pinea while Jim continued to run Fonthill.

The choice, then, was the same as it had been when they left. They could either continue to live in the Cottage, or they could renovate the big house and live there. They decided on the big house, even though renovating it would be an enormous job.

Aunt Flory had lived there all her life and had been alone for the last fifty years, so that now the house was like a Victorian museum. 'I don't think my aunt had ever moved anything in all that time. There were even peacock feathers in the hall. I see the houses that have been done up now, and some that the National Trust have done are very beautiful. But I don't think that they were ever in such perfect taste in the old days. I went into quite a few old houses in my time and people were not so conscious of how they looked then. They simply used the furniture they had, so that a very good piece that somebody had once brought out from England might be next to something bought later from the local furniture shop.'

Not only had Aunt Flory never moved anything, she had never thrown anything away either. One of the rooms, next to a spare bedroom called the Hermitage, had been used by Aunt Flory's sister

Constance. It was still known as Aunt Constance's room even though she left for England before the turn of the century and had never returned. The drawers in the chest still contained her letters, her school books, and even her Christmas cards.

On the other side of the house a suite of rooms had been used by Edgar Deane, brother-in-law of William Pitt Faithfull. Edgar Deane had not been there for over fifty years, but his rooms were still just as he had left them.

Even when Aunt Flory was too old to go upstairs, she still knew where everything was. 'If she wanted me to get something for her, she would tell me which room to go to and then to look in the middle drawer on the left-hand side of the dressing table. And sure enough, it would be there.'

Before she died, Aunt Flory had told Bobbie that she had left an awful lot of things which she should have sorted out. 'I told her not to worry. She was too old to do it then. But, my goodness, when she died I saw what she meant.'

Even in 1952 the house itself still functioned as it had during most of the time Aunt Flory had lived there. The service areas were still lit by kerosene lamps, while the front part used gas from the plant in the garden. The kitchen was still out at the back, connected to the main part of the house by a verandah covered with corrugated iron. The only sink was in the scullery next door, together with the copper and its wood fire which produced the hot water.

Some of the main bedrooms were still in the old part of the house, the part that William Pitt had built when he first took up Springfield. They were reached by walking along another covered verandah outside the back of the house, and from there a flight of stairs went up the outside wall to a door on the first floor. In the 1850s Aunt Flory as a child had been carried by her nurse up the same stairs, and had been frightened by the sudden appearance of one of the last Aborigines in the district, an old man who occasionally sat beneath a big fig tree in one corner of the courtyard. Even the fig tree was still there.

Those upstairs rooms, where most of the Faithfull children had been born, contained one of the two main bathrooms in the big house. The other was at the top of the stairs near the Hermitage and still contained the copper that had been used to provide hot water before it was replaced by the larger one in the scullery.

That bathroom could also be entered by a covered balcony which ran outside the house above the dining room windows and which gave access to the other bedrooms at the front of the house. From there, another, grander staircase led down to a lobby near the dining room. A door from that lobby led into the main hall of the house which was just inside the front door. It was this route that had provided Bobbie and her friends with such excitement when they were children.

On one side of the hall was Aunt Flory's sitting room, the library, while on the other side was the big drawing room which had a separate entrance from the garden. This room had been hardly used during Bobbie's lifetime, although it had always been kept spotless. 'My mother used to say that the two cleanest places in the whole of Goulburn were Aunt Flory's house and the gaol.'

At the back of the drawing room a door gave on to the smoking room, which could also be entered from the lobby by the dining room. Behind the smoking room, but not entered from it, was an area immediately under Mr Deane's rooms which consisted of a store room and two maid's rooms. 'Those rooms must have been very dark and damp. I remember once saying to Aunt Flory how terrible they were, but she said the maids had been very grateful to have them at all. She said it was the first time most of them had ever had a bed to themselves. But they looked awful to me.'

This area opened on to one side of the courtyard, and the maids' bathroom was on the far side, next to the scullery. Beyond the maids' rooms, and under the main bedrooms, was the dairy and the laundry.

So in 1952 this house of some thirty or forty rooms still needed fires to heat the water, kerosene for the lamps, and gas from the garden. There were only two main bathrooms and the main bedrooms could be entered only from outside. The kitchen was a long walk from the house and still used a wood stove, so that anybody needing a late night cup of tea had to light a fire first. And the only telephone was still in the box on the back verandah.

The huge garden around the house was not much better and had flourished on a 'live and let live' basis, in spite of the attentions of four gardeners. Creeper grew up the tower of the house and dense shrubs were jumbled together at the foot of the walls and extended from there into the garden. 'It had turned into a fairly tidy jungle by then. The shrubs were so close to the house that I used to hide in them when I was a child and listen to what people were saying in the drawing room.'

A winding path led to the summer house, and behind that was the gas plant. The shrubs and trees were so dense that it was impossible to see any of the house from there, even though it was only a few metres away.

'My aunt was a marvellous person, but she was funny about one thing. She would never cut a branch off anything, so they just kept getting bigger. She was the sort of person who would prop up a dead tree.'

15

Renovating the Big House

IN 1951 BOBBIE and Irwin started to make their plans for the enormous job of renovating the big house. The first thing they decided was that the need was not so much to preserve it as to make it suitable to live in. 'We did not want to restore it as a Victorian house. In fact, we didn't need to do that because that is what it still was. We knew that we would have to change much of it to make it useable, but at the same time we wanted to keep all that was worth keeping.' It was not an easy aim.

It was also beyond the scope of unskilled workmen. Specialists would need to be brought from Sydney and they would need to work to accurate drawings and carefully prepared specifications.

After developing their own ideas, by the middle of the year Bobbie and Irwin brought in a Sydney architect to refine them and to prepare for the work to start. The plan that emerged was not radical, but it met the aims they had set.

The wall that separated the front hall from the lobby of the dining room would be removed, so that the hall would become bigger and the staircase would lead directly from it. Bobbie had doubts about this because it would mean that the staircase would then be visible from the front door. But the architect persuaded her that the new hall

would look much better than the present small one. She later agreed that he had been quite right.

The library on the left of the hall would be converted into an office for Irwin, and it would be provided with a door at the end so that it could be entered directly from the side of the house.

The drawing room across the hall did not require much structural change but it was to be completely redecorated. 'I had always wanted to decorate a room around a single picture, using it as a centrepiece. I saw it done very well in one of those houses in London that you could go through. There was only one picture in that room, a Constable I think, and the rest of the room had been done to match it. It really showed the picture off beautifully and it seemed much better than all the clutter that was in the drawing room then. When I look in the magazines now it seems that clutter is coming back again, but at that time we thought it was terrible. So when we were in London we bought a picture by Algernon Newton at that year's Royal Academy in case we did decide to do the place up. It was a landscape and when the interior designer came to do the drawing room he was very clever in the way he used the same colours as the painting.'

The smoking room was to be extended so that the outside wall would be in line with that of the drawing room, and french doors would replace the small window in the existing wall. 'You could never see out of those small windows because they were so high off the ground.'

Behind the smoking room, the store area and the maids' bedrooms were to be converted into a billiard room which would house the full-size table they had brought from Fonthill. From there, a new staircase would lead up to the rooms that Edgar Deane had used. A door from the upper landing would also lead into what had been the main bedrooms, so that they could then be entered from inside the house.

But the main changes were to be on the other side of the house. The outside kitchen was no longer practical and it was decided that a new kitchen would be built near the dining room in what had been the church room. 'We worried about that. We thought it was awful to make the old church room into a kitchen, but we didn't see where else we could put it.' This kitchen was to be fitted with a new stove and a new hot water system, both of which would use oil instead of wood.

This also meant that they could now remove the covered verandahs that had led from the old kitchen and the main bedrooms and replace them with a pergola at the rear of the house.

On the first floor of the main part of the house the bathroom next to the Hermitage was to be modernised and closed off from the outside balcony. A new bathroom was to be built to serve the bedrooms at the top of the main staircase. The balcony could then be removed and the first floor of that part of the house would then consist of two separate sections, each with its own staircase.

Two factors now came into play which were of tremendous importance. The first was that it was now possible to connect Springfield to the main electricity supply from Goulburn. The cost was high because of the distance from the main road, but that cost was offset against the future cost of the electricity itself. This meant that the whole of the house could now be wired for electricity. The gas and kerosene lamps could be replaced by electric lights, labour-saving appliances could be installed in the kitchen, the laundry and elsewhere, and the entire house could be heated by electric radiators.

The second factor was that Diana was to be married the following year, and the house had to be finished by then.

It seemed hardly possible. Apart from the structural alterations, the whole of the plumbing had to be renewed, and the entire house had to be wired for electricity as well.

But what had emerged was a very thoughtful design. Apart from replacing worn ironwork, the exterior of the front and side of the house was unchanged except for the slight alteration to the wall of the smoking room. Inside, the beautiful cedar doors would either stay where they were or be used elsewhere, the ceilings would be unchanged, and even the functions of the main rooms would remain the same. But by altering the way they gave on to each other their use would be much more practical. The kitchen and other service areas would be modernised and no longer need a massive staff to make them function. In short, the house would be infinitely more comfortable for all who lived and worked in it.

The architect drew up the first specification in August 1951 and it ran to nine closely typed foolscap pages. The quote of the builder alone was for more than £25,000, at a time when a large house on Sydney's North Shore could be bought for much less than that.

Work started shortly afterwards. Tradesmen came from Sydney and lived in part of the house while they worked on the rest, and Bobbie and Irwin continued to live in the Cottage.

It was not long before Irwin thought the work was going too slowly and he said to Bobbie that he didn't think the men were working properly. 'Well, he was very good at running a station, but I didn't think he knew much about building. So I said I thought it would be better if he didn't rush in, even though we did want the place finished in time for Diana's wedding.'

But not long afterwards she accidentally overheard a conversation when one of the men used the telephone they had installed for their use and which was an extension of the phone from the Cottage. One voice said, 'I thought you said this was a good job?' and another replied, 'Yes, it was. But the owner's woken up and it's a brute of a job now.' After that it became even worse as Irwin supervised almost every aspect of it each day.

Unfortunately not all the workmen were honest either. Or at least one of them wasn't. Because each room had to be wired for electricity it was impossible to keep them locked all the time, even though they might need little other work on them. One night the foreman came over to the Cottage in great distress to say that one of his men had disappeared and some things were missing. When they checked they could not find a very old and elegant work basket, two hall chairs made of oak, and another chair that was a genuine Sheraton. They were never recovered.

As the work progressed, Bobbie was faced with the huge task of clearing out the things that would no longer be needed. Much of it was accumulated junk that had built up over the years, but the rest Irwin proposed to include in what was likely to be one of the biggest garage sales in Australian history.

But it was not as easy as that. Bobbie kept finding things that were of no direct use, but which were too personal to sell. 'We can't sell that chair. That's the one my aunt always used. And we can't sell those books because they once belonged to William Pitt.' Irwin's answer was simple, or so he thought. 'Well, put them in a museum then,' he said. Bobbie thought that was a very good idea. But not any museum. Why not, she said half jokingly, start a museum of their own?

They decided to use Edgar Deane's rooms. They did not need them for anything else, and they had the advantage of being almost a museum already.

Edgar Deane had been very keen on trotting and the walls were covered with engravings of horses that he had cut out of American

The Springfield homestead today.

magazines. So they left those where they were and Bobbie started to move in all the things that they could not use but which were part of the history of Springfield.

It soon turned into a massive collection. Apart from the furniture, there were Victorian dresses in boxes with Bond Street labels, button up boots, veils and pretty bonnets covered with lace and flowers. There were black silk top hats and silver canes and old guns and shooting sticks. And there were letters and diaries and ledgers and lists and bank accounts which went right back to the foundation of Springfield.

There was, indeed, far too much for two small rooms and some time later an expert from Canberra examined the collection and selected the most important items so that they could be made more widely available, and more professionally cared for, in the National Library. The material she selected filled two large furniture trucks, and what was left still filled Edgar Deane's rooms.

Irwin, meanwhile, had started to clear the garden. Ruthlessly. He and another man got up on a bulldozer and before long they had knocked down the summer house and had built a great pile of trees and shrubs as well as a complete rockery. 'I wanted it done, but I couldn't bear to watch it. It was practically murder. He kept saying, "This will look marvellous when I've finished with it." But when he had finished there was just a bare space.'

The house was finished just in time for Diana's wedding, which was the first to be held at Springfield itself since before the turn of the century. The garden was still unfinished, however, but that did not matter. They erected a large marquee, and the space that was left was covered with artificial grass.

The wedding was as successful as Bobbie's had been nearly thirty years earlier, and social behaviour had not changed very much since then. But by the time her grandchild married in 1978 the changes since the days of the Terranna Ball were very noticeable indeed. 'One man had too much to drink and he went to sleep on the floor. Everybody else just stepped over him. And the girls were dancing around with their eyes closed and kissing in the middle of the dance floor. I said to Diana that I thought that looked very forward and she said that at least they didn't go out and sit in cars as we had. So I didn't say anything after that!'

With the wedding over, the rest of the garden could be completed. The main job was to lay a new lawn, a vast sweep of fine turf that formed a large circle at the side of the house. The size and location of the lawn was a matter of some importance, as it would have a great bearing on the appearance of the house. 'I thought it was laid out by the architect, but Irwin said, "Not at all. I thought of that." And then Jimmy said quietly, "I thought that was my idea." I suppose they all thought of it at the same time, but it was the architect who made the final measurements.'

On the other side of the drive a swimming pool was built with the money won by Alinga, and a small plaque was set into the surrounding wall to commemorate his memory.

By the time the work was finished, the house and garden was a showpiece. The drive ran through an avenue of huge trees and then suddenly opened up into the vast sweep of lawn to reveal the large house on the other side. It had not been possible to see the house like this for as long as anybody could remember.

Inside, the rooms retained all the elegance of their original design. Timber had been refurbished, curtains and carpets replaced, and the early chandelier that could never be converted to gas had now been wired for electricity and hung from the ceiling of the drawing room. And from the large, new windows one looked, not on a mass of shrubbery, but across the lawn to the large trees that lined the drive, and beyond them to the rising paddocks of Springfield.

16

Golden Springfield

W HEN BOBBIE and Irwin moved into the big house in 1952 they were the first owners of Springfield to live there since her grandfather, William Pitt, had died in 1896.

The renovated house attracted a great deal of attention and several magazines carried illustrated articles about it. The house represented a lifestyle that was far removed from that of most of their readers'. Here were spacious rooms, sweeping staircases, beautiful pictures and valuable furniture, and its rural setting had little in common with the suburbia that most Australians knew.

While the elegance was obvious and substantial, and never failed to impress visitors, Springfield continued to be a working sheep station, just as it always had been. The wealth and welfare of those who lived there came from the sheep's back, and nobody forgot that for one moment.

The work at Springfield was little different to that of any merino stud. Ewes were mated, lambs were born, rams were classed and some sold, and every November the shearers arrived to work in the old brick woolshed near the Cottage. When they had finished, a whole year's work at Springfield was made tangible in the stacks of wool bales that would soon be shipped to the sales. From there most would be sent overseas to textile manufacturers in England, Italy, France, America

The coach house and harness room.

and Japan and the produce of Springfield would become part of Australia's valuable export trade.

With the shearing over, Christmas could be celebrated in style. The school children gave their concert in the shed, and a few days later the same shed was used for the Springfield Christmas party. 'By the time you included families and a few people who had retired, we always had about a hundred people every year. It made you realise how many people depended on the place and how big your responsibility really was.'

The highlight of the party was the arrival of Father Christmas. 'We used to get all the children to stand around the tree and sing carols so they wouldn't see him come in. It was a great moment when they realised he had arrived.' One year, after a fireplace had been installed in the shed, Bobbie told them that this year Father Christmas would come down the chimney. 'I thought they would all rush to the fireplace and look up the chimney, but not a bit of it. They all stood there like stunned mullets and the gardener who I had asked to make a noise on the roof was still stamping around when Father Christmas came in through the door. I said that it was his reindeer making the noise, but I decided not to change it again. It seemed to work very well as it was!'

After Bobbie and Irwin had moved into the house they then had to decide what to do with the Cottage. It had served them well, but now they could see no further use for it. The slate roof was in need of extensive repair and the rest of the house was not much better than the big house had been when they had started work on that. There seemed little point in preserving it, but it was now a very large house and it could not be made to disappear, or so they thought.

But it seems it could. A man arrived and offered to demolish the Cottage for no payment if he could sell the materials and fittings it contained. 'And that is what he did. Irwin said he had to promise to take everything away even if he couldn't sell it, and the man was very good about that. He found that he couldn't sell the bluestone that made up the front walls of the house and we were worried about that for a time because there was such a lot. But he buried it all in the garden — I suppose somebody will find it one day and wonder what it was for. I asked him to leave one stone which had been over one of the windows and he put it in the paddock as a seat. I think of it as a memorial of where I was born.'

Apart from that, there is now no trace of the Cottage.

Bobbie was now middle-aged and, in contrast to those earlier years, her life was fairly quiet. Her children were grown up and she and Irwin lived alone in the big house. Although she still took an interest in running Springfield, and followed all its activities closely, she was not as directly involved as she had been earlier. There were still parties, of course, but most of their social life now centred on the picnic races and Irwin's polo.

The Goulburn Polo and Picnic Race Club had been formed a few years after the Second World War with Irwin as its chairman. It had little in common with Terranna. On the contrary, the club set out to avoid the elitism that in the end had made Terranna so unpopular in Goulburn and instead welcomed members regardless of their wealth or occupation.

The first few meetings were held on the Goulburn race course, but the facilities for spectators were very poor at that time and the course lacked the atmosphere that is such an important part of picnic racing. So in 1951 the club decided to build a race course and two polo fields on land which Irwin made available at Springfield. It was a large job but the work was completed in only a few months with voluntary labour supplied by the members and in February 1952 the club held its first picnic meeting at Springfield.

'The races and the three-day polo tournaments were really hard work, but they were great fun. Irwin was president of the club for many years and so I was always involved a great deal. At the races the owners of horses, and their wives, trainers and jockeys, were all entertained to lunch in the president's tent, while other members entertained each other in their own tents. The station staff spent a lot of time making sure everything was in good order for these events, and their wives always helped with the catering.'

When Irwin retired as president in the early 1960s Jim Bell, who later became chairman of the Australian Jockey Club, took over the racing and Jim Maple-Brown took over the polo. The annual polo tournament is still held at Springfield, but in 1986 the races were moved back to a vastly improved Goulburn race course.

It was probably because of the polo that Bobbie and Irwin were invited to dinner at Government House in Canberra by the Governor-General, Sir William Slim.

'We were both very surprised. Irwin said it was all my fault, but I couldn't see how it had anything to do with me at all. Sir William had been here for the polo when Irwin was president, so I think that's how it came about.'

Irwin said they would dress at their hotel in Canberra, although Bobbie would have preferred to dress at Springfield. But as it turned out, it was as well that Irwin had his way. 'When we were driving to Canberra we got caught up with a huge flock of sheep that were on the road. The drover who was with them was pretty hopeless and in the end Irwin got out of the car and moved the sheep for him. He had to, otherwise we would never have reached Canberra on time. I said to him that he would have looked very funny doing that if he had been wearing his tails!'

Although Bobbie had been to Government House several times she found that the customs there had changed once again. 'When it was time for the ladies to withdraw, Lady Slim got up and we all did the same. She turned in the doorway and curtseyed, but the rest of us had no idea what we were supposed to do. I found out later that we were supposed to have a partner on the other side and that we should have turned together and curtseyed before going out. But all I did was a sort of shuffly bob that I thought must have looked terrible. I asked Irwin about it afterwards and he said he wasn't even looking at me. He said he was looking at the one dressed like an elderly mermaid because he thought she was going to fall over!'

Indeed, Bobbie regretted that they had to leave the room at all because she had been most interested in Sir William and his conversation. It was even more infuriating when Irwin spent the whole of the drive back telling her what a wonderful man Sir William was.

It was, fortunately, the start of a relationship that was to last until Sir William retired in 1960. 'I had a great admiration for him and thought he was one of the most outstanding men of his time. He seemed to like country people and was always glad to come to Springfield, although he wasn't able to do that very often. He didn't seem to like politicians very much and somebody told me that he liked to invite people from the land because it leavened the dough.'

Perhaps the most important invitation Bobbie and Irwin had was to meet the Queen during her visit to Australia in 1954, and for Bobbie the occasion contained some moments of sheer terror.

'The Queen hardly looked at me, and I don't blame her, but she had this long conversation with Irwin. She said that she remembered presenting him with a polo cup in England, and asked him whose team he had beaten. So he said it had been Lord Louis', and that was the wrong thing to say because Lord Louis was never supposed to be beaten. Her face fell a yard and then she said, "Oh, I remember. That was the time his pony sprained a spavin and he hurt his back." I was terrified that Irwin was going to disagree with her, but he said, "Oh, yes. I think it must have been." But he had never heard of it before.'

There was worse to come. A little later the Queen said she understood Irwin was a farmer. It was not a term he would have used and Bobbie waited for the consequences. 'I suppose we are all farmers now, but we weren't then. My father would have been frightfully insulted, you know. The term was grazier. They thought they were like those people in England with the estates, you know. They weren't farmers, and neither were the American ranch owners.'

The old flour mill. While Irwin was prepared to agree that they had beaten Lord Louis because he had been having a bad day, he was not prepared to agree that he was a farmer. No, he said, he was not a farmer. 'Well, where do you live?' she asked. 'We live on a station,' he said, and the conversation came to an end in complete confusion.

In spite of this Irwin was impressed by the Queen and complained afterwards that he thought it dreadful that she had been kept waiting at one point. Bobbie replied that Irwin himself had been known to keep people waiting on more than one occasion.

Irwin had never been an enthusiastic traveller and it seemed to Bobbie that were were unlikely to make many more trips together. Then in 1960, to her amazement, he said that they would go for a holiday. Not overseas this time, but to the back of Bourke. Literally.

Irwin had read that you could shoot pigs there, and that the fishing was also very good. Suddenly, they were the two things he wanted to do more than anything else.

They bought a station wagon so they could sleep in it, and loaded it with guns and fishing rods and everything else they could think of.

They even had an inflatable boat that was supposed to be unsinkable. By the time they left they could probably have survived anywhere in Australia for months on end.

When they reached Bourke the town was deserted because everybody had gone to the races at Louth. When Irwin did find somebody they said it would be better if they went to Louth too. Then all they had to do was flag down the first car they saw and whoever was driving would be sure to let them on their place.

'Well, one car went past, but we didn't like to flag it down so we drove on to Louth. The place was covered in bottles from the races the day before, but Irwin was able to get some local advice at the pub. They told us we could go on to a place and camp by the river.'

That afternoon they went rowing in the inflatable boat before starting the serious business of fishing the next day.

'I was rowing and Irwin was fishing. Then suddenly his line went tight and started to go down, and so did we. Then we came up again and the boat started to spin round and round. I said to him, "You know, your bottom is only just out of the water," and he shushed me and said, "This is the most exciting thing I have ever done. Anyway, this boat is unsinkable." And with that he suddenly disappeared. The back of the boat went down with him sitting in it. So I jumped out and eventually landed on the far bank of the river. By that time he had come up again and was still in the middle of the river clinging to the boat. Every time he tried to climb in it went down again, but eventually he managed to climb in over the back and started to paddle with his hands towards the other bank. So I called out, "Hey, what about me on the far side of the Darling? I can't swim the whole river." No, he said, he thought he had better come back for me. I was sixty years old then and I didn't think I could swim that far!'

Irwin had lost all his fishing gear in the river so they went into Louth the next day to replace it. 'But there was absolutely nothing there, and Irwin was so disgusted that we packed up and came home. We were only away for a week.'

It was their last trip together. In 1963 they discovered that Irwin Maple-Brown had cancer and he died the following year. He and Bobbie had been married for forty years.

'I found it very difficult. My mother had died in 1959 and suddenly there seemed to be nobody left. There were the children, of course, but they were living their own lives and I didn't want to be a nuisance to them. So I just went on living in the big house on my own and Jimmy took over the running of Springfield. Life goes on, you know, even though you don't know how you are going to manage. But life is never the same. The contentment seems to go out of it.'

17

Since Then

IN 1965, A YEAR after Irwin's death, Bobbie went to England on her own.

'It wasn't quite the same as when I was there in 1950 with Irwin and Diana. They always wanted to be somewhere where they would see a horse, you know, so we had to go to all the shows. I enjoy them when I am with somebody who likes them, but it is not something I would really do on my own.'

Instead, she hired a car and spent most of the time wandering around England.

'I still loved the country. I feel quite sorry for the young ones now when they travel. It is so much easier to do and I think it is marvellous that so many young people can go and see these places for themselves. But I think they miss something. We had read all the books about England and it was almost as if we had dropped into a fairy tale.'

She returned by sea, this time by way of America. 'I found some good company on the ship and I quite enjoyed the trip. Of course, I was with the old widows by now.'

Not entirely, though. She was surprised to find herself sharing a cabin with a young American schoolgirl who told her that she had been reluctant to come on the trip because it meant leaving her boyfriend. But she didn't live with him, she said, because they thought it better to have something to look forward to, although some of her friends at school had already had babies.

'Well, I was gazing at the ceiling absolutely pop-eyed. I had never heard of all that before. She asked me what I thought and I said, "Well, I really don't know, dear, but in my day a man who was fond of you wouldn't have put you in such an awkward position." Then when I realised what I had said I couldn't help laughing, and she couldn't understand why, which made me laugh more! But it was a big shock to me. I've got used to it since then, but a schoolgirl not living with him so they would have something to look forward to! But times change. I remember saying to one of my grandchildren how romantic it was when you were outside looking at the moon, and she said it would have been before everybody knew that it was just an old rock.'

There was amusement too. One day she and the young girl left the ship to visit Everglades. It was a very hot day and the girl was 'fagged out' when they returned to the ship. 'I asked her how she would have been when they were coaling a steamer at Colombo and she said she thought she would have died. Funny how people have got used to their comfort, isn't it?'

During the following years Bobbie travelled extensively. In 1966 she went to stay on Ardmoor Station south of Mount Isa, in 1967 she went through Victoria to Adelaide and Alice Springs — 'I had promised Jim that I would not climb Ayers Rock, but I did go up as far as the handrail'. The following year she took Diana to America, and in 1969, when she was nearly seventy, she planned a motoring trip to Bourke and Moree.

When Irwin had returned from England with his Bentley, Jim had said that it would not be long before he would want to change it for something else, as Irwin rarely kept any car for more than two years. And sure enough, he did. Rather than trade the Bentley, however, Irwin suggested that Bobbie take it over and he would trade in her smaller car instead.

Bobbie enjoyed driving the Bentley, and it had another, even more important, advantage. She could always find it. When she started to plan her motoring trip, though, Jimmy suggested she replace the Bentley with something more practical. She did, but it was confusing

for a time. 'I would come out of a shop and think, heavens, somebody has stolen the Bentley. And then I would remember that I didn't have it any more. Then I would have to find my white Ford, which was difficult because there were always so many of them.'

There were other changes too. While Jim had been running Fonthill he had come to the conclusion that the traditional merino was no longer very suitable in a business that was increasingly expensive to run. So over a period of years he developed a different merino, one which could be used to produce meat as well as wool and which was far easier to look after.

This sheep looked quite different to the merino that Lucian Faithfull had known so well. It was bigger, it had no horns, and it had none of the massive folds that traditionally were so highly regarded but which made shearing difficult and which also provided a breeding ground for flies.

Because it looked so different this new merino was not very popular, but Jim was convinced that it was an innovation that the wool industry badly needed. It was time, he thought, to bring these sheep down from Fonthill and to breed them at Springfield instead of the traditional merinos that had been so famous there. It would be the end of a style of breeding that had been carried out at Springfield for over a hundred years.

'When Jim first showed me a picture of one of his rams I said that it looked like a decent wether. But he gave me a copy of the book that explained it all and asked me to read it because I don't think he wanted to make such a big change unless I agreed with it. So I started reading the book when I went to bed, and by midnight I saw what he was doing. I thought I couldn't ring him at that time to tell him that I agreed with him, but he probably would have been glad if I had. I think you have to change, even though the old ways might have been good in their day. But so many old families seem to sit around doing nothing, and complaining because everything has altered. You might have been very fond of wooden ships, but once the others came in there would have been no use going on with them, would there?'

Bobbie continued to live in the big house alone, just as Aunt Flory had, but it was now much more comfortable than it had been then.

'It might have seemed silly, living in that huge place, but I really would not have liked to move. Anyway, the others were all bringing up children and that house never was very good for that. When my grandchildren came over they would go off to play somewhere in the house and you never knew where they were. It could take half an hour to find them!'

It was not until 1982 that she felt ready to make the move. In a meticulously planned sequence, Bobbie moved out of the big house into a renovated cottage nearby. It had once been a gardener's cottage and had been the home of the English nurse who had been with them in England in 1901. At the same time, Jim and Pam moved into the house, while his son Richard and his wife Sue moved into their house at Pinea.

'I just knew by then that it was the right thing to do for all of us.'

Epilogue

BOBBIE MAPLE-BROWN is now eighty-six years old and she still lives in her cottage at Springfield only a few hundred metres from where she was born. She is looked after by Elvy McClelland, who was born on Springfield in 1915 where her mother had been a parlour maid at the Cottage. Elvy started doing housework at the Cottage in 1944 and she has been with Bobbie ever since.

Bobbie plays bridge once a week, reads almost constantly, and spends the rest of her time knitting. 'Well, I was always quite a good knitter, I thought. But one day the Children's Home advertised for woollen jumpers and I decided to knit one for them. So in due course I rang the bell at the home and said to the girl who came that I had brought them this jumper. "Oh," she said, "thank you so much. We have a wonderful woman who can undo it and knit it into a beautiful new jumper." I think I did say in a squeak that I had only just finished it, but I don't think she heard me!'

Bobbie's only problem is that she now has arthritis in her knees and has difficulty moving. 'But it is all right if I sit here like an ancient monument and people come to see me.'

They do so frequently. Jim and Pam walk across nearly every evening and Richard and Sue drop in often during the week. When they are all there, they represent three successive generations of the

Faithfull Maple-Browns that have run Springfield. Only the first two, William Pitt Faithfull and Lucian Faithfull, are missing.

Springfield is still as impressive and as successful as it ever was. It now covers about 7,500 acres (3,000 hectares) and runs 14,000 Fonthill merinos bred by Jim Maple-Brown. In Lucian Faithfull's day the property was worked by a small army, and even after the war Irwin employed twenty men. Springfield now employs three men and a jackeroo, and that is an indication of the benefits of the 'easy care' sheep that are now synonymous with Springfield.

Most of the buildings that Bobbie knew as a child are still there. The cottages that were once used by the station hands are now mostly let to people who work in Goulburn. There is no longer a school on Springfield, but the old buildings still stand, as do all the buildings around the village square. Aunt Flory's coach is still kept in the coach house, its paintwork just as Brewsters finished it in 1888. All it needs is two horses and somebody with the old skill of driving them.

Bobbie Maple-Brown is at ease with herself, comfortable in her old age among the surroundings she knows so well,

'I really have had a fortunate life, you know. I would not have changed any of it.'